BARBIE,

HAMAS, AND

OPPENHEIMER

BARBIE, HAMAS, AND OPPENHEIMER

DENIED, DEGRADED, AND DISTORTED VERSIONS OF THE UNIVERSE: A LOVE STORY

THE DENIAL OF "KEN AND BARBIE" IS A DIRECT CAUSE OF EXISTENTIAL RISK

. . .

One Mountain, Many Paths: Oral Essays

Volume 28

DR. MARC GAFNI

Author: Marc Gafni
Title: Barbie, Hamas, and Oppenheimer

Identifiers: ISBN 979-8-88834-015-8 (electronic)
ISBN 979-8-88834-014-1 (paperback)
Library of Congress Cataloging-in-Publication Data available

Edited by Krista Josepha Steenbergen and Kathy Brownback

World Philosophy and Religion Press,
St. Johnsbury, VT

in conjunction with

IP Integral Publishers

https://worldphilosophyandreligion.org

JOIN THE REVOLUTION!

CONTENTS

CHAPTER 4   THE MOCKING OF THE HERO

CHAPTER 5   "THE UNIVERSE: A LOVE STORY" IN THE MOUTH OF PATRIARCHY

CHAPTER 13   *BARBIE*, HAMAS & *HOMO AMOR*—FROM DEGRADED LOVE STORIES TO THE UNIVERSE: A LOVE STORY

EDITORIAL NOTE ABOUT AUTHORSHIP, EDITING, AND THE RADICAL CONTEXT FOR THIS SERIES

ORAL ESSAYS FROM THE ONE MOUNTAIN, MANY PATHS WEEKLY BROADCAST

This volume is part of the Oral Essays library, a series of lightly edited, compiled transcripts of oral teachings given by Dr. Marc Gafni in the weekly online broadcast, *One Mountain, Many Paths*. Originally called an "Evolutionary Church," *One Mountain, Many Paths* became a key venue for the articulation of an inspired and deeply grounded new Story of Value in response to the meta-crisis. Marc—together with Zak Stein,[1] Kristina Kincaid, Ken Wilber, Sally Kempton, Barbara Marx Hubbard, Lori Galperin, Aubrey Marcus and dozens of other thought-leaders over the years—began to articulate what they call a World Philosophy and World Religion[2] as a context for our diversity.

---

1 Zak, together with Ken Wilber, has been Marc's primary intellectual partner and an initiate lineage holder in CosmoErotic Humanism.

2 This project is grounded in four core organizational frameworks: 1) The Center for World Philosophy and Religion, co-founded by Marc Gafni, Zachary Stein, Sally Kempton, and Ken Wilber, and chaired over the years by John P. Mackey, Barbara Marx Hubbard, Aubrey Marcus, Gabrielle Anwar and Shareef Malnik, Carrie Kish and Adam Bellow, and Kathleen J. Brownback. 2) The Office for the Future, chaired by Stephanie Valcke and Ivan Bossyut. 3) The World Philosophy and Religion Press, founded and chaired by Aubrey Marcus, together with Marc Gafni and Zachary Stein. 4) The Foundation for Conscious Evolution, founded by Barbara Marx Hubbard and currently chaired by Peter Fiekowsky. For a complete list of key leadership, see the Office for the Future website, www.officeforthefuture.com.

Much of the *dharma* material in this editorial note comes directly from Marc, so it was originally all in quotation marks—but that looked a little odd. So per his suggestion we removed them, and the reader should consider the paragraphs on the next several pages as one extended quote from him. We are joyfully grateful to Marc for the clarity of his *dharma*, the elegance and "second simplicity" of this language, and the mad, Outrageous Love with which he transmits his teachings.

Barbara and Marc called the mission of *One Mountain* "a Planetary Awakening in Evolutionary Love Through Unique Self Symphonies." We are an evolutionary community with a deeply grounded, radically alive, and "post-tragic" revolutionary spirit. We are activating a new humanity and awakening as a new species: *Homo amor*, the fulfillment of *Homo sapiens*.

One Mountain is committed to articulating a Story of Value that can become the ground for the new society that must be birthed in response to the meta-crisis. We recognize that we are living at a pivotal moment in history. In this "time between stories," the great moral imperative is to tell the new Story of Value. It is ours to do, personally and collectively, with great trembling and ecstatic joy.

FROM DOGMA TO DHARMA: ETERNAL AND EVOLVING FIRST PRINCIPLES AND FIRST VALUES

The teachings are grounded in decades of deep study across many wisdom traditions. Over the years, week by week, these teachings were incrementally developed within the framework of the *One Mountain, Many Paths* broadcast. We often refer to these teachings as *dharma*.

This word was originally used in lineage traditions to refer to something like universal law. This is a crucial realization: just as there is universal law in mathematical value, there is also a sense of universal law in ethics and value.

Historically, dharma often devolved into unchanging dogma. Evolution was ignored, and the natural process of dharma evolution became disconnected from its deep, eternal context. The weakness of the word dharma is that too often it did not include the evolving insights of the sciences, it confused local cultural truths with universal truths, and it used words like "eternal," as in "eternal Tao," as opposed to words like "evolution."

Eternal came to mean unchanging, and that kind of thinking often led to overly ethnocentric readings of dharma. Local systems would claim their religious and cultural insights as immutable, which stood in the way of the emergence of a genuine world Story of Value that is real, inherent to Cosmos, and backed by the Universe—even as it is also always evolving.

Or, as we often say, "eternal value is evolving value. The eternal Tao is the evolving Tao."

We have shown that, emergent from profound insights in the "interior sciences," eternal does not mean unchanging in time; it means what we call the deeper Field of ErosValue that is beneath culture, geography, and history, which lives beneath all individual and collective values, and beneath time and space itself.

As such, we have gradually transitioned from the term dharma to the term *Value*, in the sense of the Field of Value that lives beneath all values. This Field of Value discloses as First Principles and First Values embedded in a Story of Value.

Indeed, as the interior sciences knew and the exterior sciences imply, Reality arises in a Field of ErosValue in which an entire set of mathematical, musical, molecular, moral, and mystical values are the very ground of all being. That Field of Value is eternal—the true ground of the Good, True and Beautiful—even as it is evolving.

But of course, it is equally critical not just to talk about evolving value, but to ground the evolving value in its true nature, the eternal Field of First

Principles and First Values, always reaching for ever-more life, ever-more love, ever-more care, ever-more depth, ever-more uniqueness, ever-more intimate communion, and ever-more transformation.

As such, when we refer to the word dharma, which still appears in these texts together with the word value, we refer to an evolving dharma grounded in an *eternal and evolving* Field of Value. Indeed, eternity and evolution are two faces of the whole, opposites joined at the hip, that characterize the nature of our Cosmos in virtually all of its expressions.

It's in these terms that we ground a robust world philosophy that integrates the validated, leading-edge insights of premodern traditional wisdom, modern wisdom, and more recent postmodern insights, weaving them together into a new whole greater than the sum of its parts.

This new whole is a shared Story of Value rooted in First Principles and First Values that are both eternal and evolving.

These First Principles and First Values of Cosmos are woven together into a new Story of Value as a context for our diversity, a new Universe Story. This new Story gives us the best possible responses we have to the mystery, and to the great questions:

- Who am I? Who are we?
- Where am I? Where are we?
- What should I do? What should we do?

It is only through such a shared Universe Story—a narrative of identity and ethos as a context for our blessed diversity—that we can realize how what unites is so much greater than what divides us.

Only a new Story of Value will allow us to both respond to the meta-crisis and participate together in birthing the most true, good, and beautiful world that we already know is possible.

THIS ORAL ESSAYS SERIES IS AN ENTRYWAY TO THE GREAT LIBRARY OF COSMOEROTIC HUMANISM

This Oral Essays series is part of the overarching project of the Great Library at the Center for World Philosophy and Religion, led by Dr. Marc Gafni, together with Dr. Zak Stein. The aim of the Great Library project is to articulate a robust and comprehensive new Story of Value, CosmoErotic Humanism, in the form of dozens of well-researched and extensively footnoted academic works.

Our vision is to provide the philosophical framework that will be vital for navigating humanity through this time of immense crisis and transformation.

To begin your journey into CosmoErotic Humanism, we tenderly refer you to the book *First Principles and First Values*, co-authored by Marc Gafni, Zak Stein, and Ken Wilber, under the name David J. Temple. David J. Temple is a pseudonym created for enabling ongoing collaborative authorship at the Center for World Philosophy and Religion. The two primary authors behind David J. Temple are Marc Gafni and Zak Stein, and for different projects, specific writers will be named as part of the collaboration, such as Ken Wilber and others.

Three other volumes complete this introduction: *A Return to Eros*, by Marc Gafni and Kristina Kincaid; *Your Unique Self*, by Marc Gafni; and *Education in a Time between Worlds*, by Zak Stein.

We hope that the Oral Essays in the present volume, with their informal style of transmission, will serve as an allurement and entryway for you into the more formal books of the Great Library that provide the robust intellectual underpinnings of the new Story of Value.

A NOTE ABOUT THE EDITORS

This Oral Essays collection has been edited by students of the new Story of CosmoErotic Humanism. Each of us has actively participated in *One*

Mountain, Many Paths, and most of us have been in deep "Holy of Holies" study with Dr. Marc Gafni for many years.

We have been privileged to find ourselves well-versed in the teachings, and even emerging as lineage-holders of CosmoErotic Humanism.[3]

We view this editing project as a privilege and a deep practice of study and clarification. We experience ourselves as a *mystical editing society*, frequently meeting and conversing together about the content—the depth of knowledge and wisdom offered here—as well as the technical intricacies involved with publishing a beautiful and coherent series of books. In so doing, we function as a "Unique Self Symphony," which itself is a Dharmic term that connotes an omni-considerate collaboration between realized Unique Selves synergizing our unique gifts into a new emergence greater than the sum of the parts. Even as we worked diligently to standardize our editing styles, meeting on a weekly basis to debate the nuances of phrasing, we also operated from within a deep appreciation of the unique style that

---

3 CosmoErotic Humanism is a world philosophical movement aimed at reconstructing the collapse of value at the core of global culture. Much like Romanticism or Existentialism, CosmoErotic Humanism is not merely a theory but a movement that changes the very mood of Reality. It is an invitation to participate in evolving the source code of consciousness and culture towards a cosmocentric ethos for a planetary civilization.

The term CosmoErotic Humanism, initially coined by Dr. Gafni and colleagues, points to a complex, multi-faceted, layered, and nuanced evolutionary set of insights that has evolved over decades of intensive research, teaching, and spiritual practice from deep within a wide range of wisdom traditions (including the Wisdom of Solomon lineage tradition, Bodhisattva Buddhism, and Kashmir Shaivism), as well as multiple disciplines including complexity theory, chaos theory, emergence theory, molecular biology, and the more classical disciplines of the humanities.

The seeds of CosmoErotic Humanism were planted with Dr. Marc Gafni's work on a two-volume, 1,000-page opus called *Radical Kabbalah* (Integral Publishers, 2012). This scholarly work, sourced from deep study within the esoteric lineage texts of the Wisdom of Solomon, points to a non-dual, or acosmic, realization which—unlike the prevailing conceptualization of non-duality—does not efface the human being; rather, it is highly humanistic in its nature. The next step in the evolution of CosmoErotic Humanism was the insight that all of Reality is evolving Eros, which lives in, as, and through the human being.

A failure of Eros leads inexorably to the creation of narratives of "pseudo-eros." CosmoErotic Humanism is a response to the modern mental and social breakdown sourced in the proliferation of multiple forms of pseudo-eros and its broken narratives, such as rivalrous conflict governed by win/lose metrics and the dogmatic denial of intrinsic value in Cosmos, which together generate our current "global intimacy disorder."

each editor brought to his or her work. As such, the reader might notice some variation in editing style among the books.

Please note that Dr. Marc Gafni has not reviewed these edited Oral Essays, as he is deeply engaged in writing the formal books of the Great Library. But he has been generous in responding to questions and providing overall guidance in the project. Overall, as Marc's students and students of the dharma, we have made it a key project at the Center to publish these pieces of work relatively independently.

OUR UNIQUE ORAL-ESSAY EDITING STYLE PRESERVES THE ENERGY OF THE ORIGINAL TRANSMISSION

Dr. Marc Gafni is a uniquely gifted teacher whose oral transmission is imbued with a quality that has proven transformative for his students. Many of us feel mystically transformed by both the content and the underlying energy of the transmission style. Therefore, as we like to say, *trust the magic ways the dharma comes through your unique understanding!*

As Marc's empowered students, colleagues, and beloved friends, we have a deep knowing that these teachings are vital for the survival and thriving of humanity as we know it, and we recognize the importance of publishing his teachings in a written format that will be accessible by future generations. At the same time, we sought to preserve the Eros of the original oral transmission with all of its nuance, power, and depth. Our intention in the editing process, to the greatest extent possible, has been to keep these spoken artifacts intact in order to maintain the flow of the original transmission. We have therefore chosen not to engage in intensive formal editing, as we found that doing so resulted in the loss of the energetic transmission that is so key to fully receiving the *dharma*.

After experimenting with many ways to present these texts, we developed a specific way of laying out the text on the page. Marc, in collaboration with Zak Stein and Russian intellectual/artist Elena Maslova-Levin—and ultimately all of the editors, through many conversations—developed a unique, artistic presentation of the text, using bolding, italics, bullet points, and other stylistic features that together serve to accentuate the immediacy of the oral transmission.

As part of this editing style, intended to preserve the integrity of the original transmission, we have refrained from removing the frequent recapitulations of key themes. We found that each recapitulation contributes something vital to the rhythm and music beneath the words, like the beating drum of our hearts. These recapitulations not only review previous material but also add important new emphases, perspectives, and elements of the new Story of Value. We ask for your patience as a reader to trust the rhythm of these texts, and we trust you as a reader to have the depth and steadiness to find your way through.

THE INVITATION

We invite you to find your way into this revolution. Each one of our Unique Selves and unique gifts are desperately needed as we co-create this new Story of Value together, as part of the covenant between generations, for the sake of the whole.

Let's *play a larger game* and evolve the very source code of consciousness and culture together.

With mad love,

The Editors

LOVE OR DIE

LOCATING OURSELVES: ARTICULATING THE ESSENTIAL CONTEXT FOR THE ONE MOUNTAIN, MANY PATHS ORAL ESSAYS

SETTING OUR INTENTION

Intention setting is everything.

We're here—as da Vinci was with his cohort in the Renaissance—**to play a larger game, to participate in the evolution of love, which is to tell the new Story of Value rooted in First Principles and First Values.**

- Our intention is to recognize the critical historical juncture in which we find ourselves.
- Our intention is to take our seat at the table of history and to say, *we take responsibility for this.*
- Our intention is to participate as revolutionaries for the sake of the whole.

What we're here to do is revolution; revolution for the sake of the evolution of love.

It's a revolution for the sake of the trillions of unborn lives that will not manifest:

- The unborn loves
- The unborn creativity
- The unborn goodness
- The unborn truth
- The unborn beauty

All of it looks to us.

Not because we're engaged in grandiosity. Not at all!

- We're trembling before She.
- We're trembling with joy at the privilege.
- We're trembling with joy at the responsibility.
- We're trembling with joy at the Possibility of Possibility.
- We have to enact a new Story in this moment of time. Because it is only a new Story that can change the vector of history.

The most revolutionary act that we can do—the greatest moral imperative of this time—**is to articulate a new Story at this time between worlds and this time between stories.**

Story is not made up, as postmodernity suggests. **We all live in inescapable frameworks; our framework is the story we live in.** Right now, Reality lives according to win/lose metrics, a story that is generating existential risk. **We need to change that story.**

When we change that story, when we tell a new Story—not a made-up story, but a new Story of Value, rooted in First Principles and First Values—**then it all changes.**

We need to participate in the evolution of the source code of consciousness and culture, which is the evolution of love.

It's the most important, exciting, evolutionary, revolutionary act that we can do to alleviate suffering: to be lovers.

Like Rumi, the great poet of Sufism, we have to be "mad lovers," because it's the only sanity.

To be mad lovers is to see around the corner, to not be so obsessed with the details of the contractions of my life.

Let me see bigger.

Let me take complete care of myself in every possible way, let me completely attend to those in my circle of intimacy and influence, and then—*let me expand my circle.*

That's what we're here for.

- Our intention is to participate in the *LoveForce*, the *LoveIntelligence*, the *LoveBeauty*, the *LoveDesire* that literally animates Cosmos all the way up and all the way down.
- Our intention is to participate in the evolution of love.

    [*In the next few pages we will cover some key concepts which are essential to locating ourselves and setting the context for all the One Mountain, Many Paths Oral Essays.—Eds.*]

OVERVIEW: EROS IS NO LONGER A LUXURY—IT'S LOVE OR DIE

Eros is life.

The failure of Eros destroys life.

Our lack of Eros is poised to destroy the world.

All civilizations have fallen because the stories that they lived in were, in some sense, stories based on rivalrous conflict governed by win/lose metrics. Every civilization was weakened by interior polarization caused by the lack of a shared Story of Value.

We now have a global civilization, but we haven't created a shared Story of Value.

We haven't solved the generator functions that caused all civilizations to fall. Our global civilization has exponential technologies and extraction models depleting the Earth of resources that took billions of years to create, which is going to lead to a civilizational collapse.

Existential risk is risk to our very existence.

The choice is clear: love or die.

It's that simple.

Eros is no longer a luxury. It is an absolute necessity for the survival of the individual and the planet.

In the last half a century, modern psychology has documented an age-old truth: a fully nourished baby who is not held in loving arms will die.

So too, our world, both personal and global—even with all the resources of intelligence and technology at our disposal—will die without being held in love, in the embrace of Eros.

We must embrace a personal path of love and a global politics of love.

Not ordinary love. Not love which is "mere human sentiment," but Eros, or what we sometimes call Outrageous Love, which is the heart of existence itself.

We live in a world of outrageous pain.

The only response is Outrageous Love.

WHAT IS EROS?

Eros is the experience of radical aliveness, moving towards, seeking, desiring ever-deeper contact and ever-greater wholeness.[4] Eros is the core fabric of Reality's being and the motivational architecture of Reality's becoming.

Eros is what animates the evolutionary impulse itself, from the very inception of Cosmos all the way to our very selves, who awaken to the realization that the evolutionary impulse throbs uniquely in each of us.

The realization of human awakening and transformation that lies at the core of the interior sciences is the invitation—or even the urgent and desperate demand—of a madly loving Cosmos animated by infinities of power and infinities of intimacy.

The demand—the desperate invitation, the plea, the tender and fierce command of Cosmos that lives inside every human being—is to awaken: to awaken to our true nature as unique incarnations of Eros and Ethos that are needed and desperately desired by All-That-Is. Said slightly differently: Reality is Eros. Or: God is Eros.

The failure of Eros destroys life. The collapse of Eros is always the hidden (or not so hidden) root cause for the collapse of ethics.

This is true both personally and collectively. We live in a moment of a worldwide and personal collapse of Eros. Our lack of Eros is poised to destroy the world. Humanity is currently experiencing what has come to be known

---

4 We define Eros through what we refer to as the Eros equation (one of a series of what we call interior science equations):

$$Eros = Radical\ Aliveness \times Desiring\ (Growing + Seeking) \times Deeper\ Contact \times Greater\ Wholeness \times Self\ Actualization/Self\ Transcendence\ (Creation\ [Destruction])$$

There are good reasons for the formal language of the interior science equations in these writings, and the reader is invited to explore them on their own, in particular, in our work, David J. Temple, *First Principles and First Values: Forty-Two Propositions on CosmoErotic Humanism, the Meta-Crisis, and the World to Come* (World Philosophy and Religion, 2024).

as existential risk, a risk to our very existence, or what I will refer to as the Second Shock of Existence.

EXISTENTIAL RISK: THE SECOND SHOCK OF EXISTENCE

The first shock of existence is the death of the human being—the realization that we will die, which dawns in human consciousness at the beginning of history. We are not talking about the biological fact of death but the *existential* realization of death. Although the interior sciences disclose that death is a portal between two days (there is vast empirical,[5] philosophical,[6] and anthro-ontological evidence[7] for the continuity of consciousness[8]), death is also, in our own direct surface experience, a stark end. And that is obviously not a bug but a feature in the system.

---

5 We refer to evidence gathered by the most serious of researchers, beginning with Henry and Edith Sedgwick at Cambridge University and William James at Harvard University, and continuing in highly rigorous form for the last 150 years, as recapitulated by Whiteheadian scholar David Ray Griffin in multiple volumes. See also, for example, Dean Radin, *Real Magic: Unlocking Your Natural Psychic Abilities to Create Everyday Miracles* (Potter/TenSpeed/Harmony, 2018), *The Conscious Universe: The Scientific Truth of Psychic Phenomena* (HarperCollins, 2010), and other books. Or see the earlier classic by Frederic William Henry Myers, *Human Personality and Its Survival of Bodily Death* (Longmans, Green, 1907).

6 This requires a cogent analysis of materialism and dualism, and the introduction of the far more cogent third possibility which we have called "pan-interiority."

7 We discuss Anthro-Ontology in some depth in *First Principles and First Values*, and see also the fuller conversation in David J. Temple, *First Principles and First Values: Towards an Evolving Perennialism: Introducing the Anthro-Ontological Method*—both published by World Philosophy and Religion Press, in Conjunction with Integral Publishers. For now, we will simply define it as an "innate and clear interior gnosis directly available to the human being."

8 See Dr. Marc Gafni and Dr. Zachary Stein's essay in preparation, "Beyond Death: Anthro-Ontology, Philosophy, and Empiricism." This essay is slated to appear in the book *Towards a World Religion: Homo Amor Essays.* The essay is also the ground for a larger book by the same authors, *Twelve Portals to Life Beyond Death: Responding to the Second Shock of Existence,* in which we discuss three forms of material: the empirical, the philosophical, and the anthro-ontological, and show how each form discredits the notion of death as the end.

Our first-person experience is that death ends this life. It is not the *totality* of our experience if we go deeper inside, but it is obviously intended to be the central, potent, and painful dimension of every human life. Indeed, as Ernest Becker potently reminded us, the denial of death is at our peril.

All the stories and all the plotlines and all the threads of living end at that moment. Whatever happens beyond, we have an actual experience of ending. **Paradoxically, that ending, the experience of the finality of mortality, is what presses us into life.** From the implicit demand of the first shock of existence, human beings were activated and pressed into creative emergence, and what emerged was all of human culture, both interior and exterior.

The second shock of existence is the realization of the potential death of all humanity. After all the stages of human history—matter, life, and mind in all of their stages of evolutionary unfolding—we have come to this place in the evolution of humanity, in which the gap between our exponentially expanding exterior technologies and our stalled (or even regressing) interior technologies of value has created dire catastrophic and existential risks.

This gap generates extraction models and exponential growth curves, rivalrous conflicts based on win/lose metrics, tragedies of the commons, and multipolar traps, in which everyone has to keep producing to the nth degree, including weaponized exponential threats to our very existence because we are afraid that the other parties are going to do it and not be transparent—hide it from us and then dominate us.

GENERATOR FUNCTIONS FOR EXISTENTIAL RISK

Let's outline clearly the main generator functions for existential risk.

Rivalrous conflicts governed by zero-sum, win/lose metrics. Rivalrous conflicts generate extraction models at the core of the economic system and exponential growth curves. Both of these drive and are driven by a contrived system of artificially manufactured desires and needs, delivered into culture by ever more precise forms of micro-targeting to individuals and groups through the ever more immersive environment of the internet.

Next, rivalrous conflicts and exponential growth curves animated by win/lose metrics generate **complicated, fragile world systems** highly vulnerable to myriad forms of collapse. Fragile local systems are made exponentially more fragile on a global level by our inability to meet global challenges with social, legal, political, economic, and ethical infrastructures that remain largely local.

All of this is a direct result of the failure to develop more adequate interior technologies that would be sufficiently compelling to displace "rivalrous conflict governed by win/lose metrics" as the motivational architecture for the human life world.

This failure has led to the conditions that will cause the implosion of systems that are already and quite literally on the brink of collapsing themselves. That's what we mean by the second shock of existence.

To recapitulate: the second shock of existence is not the death of the human being, but the potential death of humanity.

It is the Death Star moment of our species.

THE DECONSTRUCTION OF INTRINSIC VALUE

We stand in this moment poised between utopia and dystopia, at a time between worlds and a time between stories. We need a new Story of Value, eternal yet evolving, rooted in First Principles and First Values, which would become a universal grammar of value and a context for our diversity.

This is exactly what the Renaissance was. It was a time between worlds and a time between stories. In the Renaissance, we had recently been challenged by the Black Death, a pandemic that swept across Europe. The Black Death destroyed between a third to half of Europe and a huge part of Asia.

People died horrifically, brutally, in the streets. They had no idea how to meet this challenge, and so, in response to the Black Death, da Vinci and Ficino and their cohorts understood that they had to tell a new Story of Value.

That story was the story of modernity. Did they get it right?

- They got part of it right, which birthed, to use Jürgen Habermas' phrase, "the dignities of modernity," such as new ways of gathering information and universal human rights.
- But they also deconstructed the source of Value. They lost the basis for the Good, the True, and the Beautiful.

The basis used to be divine revelation: *God told us.* But this claim was owned by religion, and every religion began to overreach and over-claim. The revelation was thus often mediated through cultural categories and wasn't fully accurate.

Modernity threw out revelation, but was unable to establish a new basis for value.

Value was just assumed to be real. As it says in the founding document of the American Revolution: *We hold these truths to be self-evident—*that is, *we don't really have a basis for value; we just take it as a given.*

In other words, modernity took out a loan of social capital from the traditional world. The source of value was never worked out.

And then, gradually, value began to collapse.

- The Universe Story began to collapse.
- The belief that the Good, the True, and the Beautiful are real began to collapse.
- The belief that Love is real began to collapse.

As Bertrand Russell is reported to have said, "I cannot see how to refute the arguments for the subjectivity of ethical values, but I find myself incapable of believing that all that is wrong with wanton cruelty is that I do not like it."

What do you do if you grew up in a world in which value is not real? A world without a source of value, without a Universe Story, without a story of human identity, without a story of desire, without a narrative of power?

In the words of W.B. Yeats, *the center does not hold*.

- You have a collapse at the very center of society, because you no longer have Eros.
- You no longer have a Reality in which value is real, and so you have this lingering sense of emptiness.
- You have a complete collapse at the very center.
- We become *the hollow men and the stuffed men*, gesture without form.

And that's the source of our current existential risk.

THE DEEPER ROOT CAUSE OF THE META-CRISIS: A GLOBAL INTIMACY DISORDER

Above, I have outlined the major generator functions of existential risk. But there is a deeper cause for the existential risk that lurks underneath the rivalrous conflict governed by win/lose metrics and the fragile systems they engender.

And we cannot take the Death Star down without discerning and addressing this. We have already alluded to this root cause above, but at this point we need to make it more explicit so that, from this context, the adequate root response will become clear.

Modernity threw out the revelation, but was unable to establish a new basis for value.

This ostensibly surprising statement can be understood in a few simple steps:

1. All of the catastrophic and existential risk challenges we face are global: from climate change to artificial intelligence, pandemics, systems collapse, and exponential arms races.
2. Every global challenge self-evidently requires a global solution.
3. Global solutions can only be implemented with global co-ordination.
4. Global co-ordination is impossible without global coherence.
5. Global coherence is only possible if there is a global resonance between the parts.
6. Global resonance is only possible if we have global intimacy.

ONLY A SHARED STORY OF VALUE CAN GENERATE GLOBAL INTIMACY

Global intimacy—just like intimacy in a couple—is only possible when there is a shared story.

Not just a shared history, but a shared Story of Value.

- It is only a shared global story that can generate a new emergent quality of intimacy: global intimacy.
- A shared Story of Value must be rooted in shared ordinating values, or what we have called evolving First Values and First Principles.
- Intimacy requires a shared grammar of value as a matrix for a shared Story of Value.

The global intimacy disorder is the root cause for existential risk. The global intimacy disorder underlies the core generator functions for existential risk.

The global intimacy disorder is rooted in the failure to experience ourselves in a field of shared intrinsic value. This failure derives from the deconstruction of value.

Indeed, it is wholly accurate to say that **the root cause of the two generator functions of existential risk is the failed story of intrinsic value, or what we might also call the breakdown of Eros.**

1. The first generator function is **the success story.** Our modern success story is rivalrous conflict governed by win/lose metrics, which violates all the terms of the Intimacy Equation: there is no shared identity and no mutuality of recognition, feeling, value or purpose, and instead of *relative* otherness, there is *alienated* otherness. Such a story generates complicated fragile systems with no allurement or intimacy between the parts, systems which optimize for efficiency (as an expression of win/lose metrics) and not for resiliency and life.

2. The second generator function is **the deconstruction of intrinsic value** itself. The deconstruction of value is the sense that human value does not participate in the intrinsic value of the Real, for the Real is dogmatically declared to have no intrinsic value. Thus, there is no shared identity between the interior of the human being and Reality. There is no common participation in a field of shared intrinsic value. Instead of being intimate with value, we are alienated from value. And only intrinsic value can arouse will: political, moral, and social will.

To sum up, without a shared grammar of value there is no global intimacy, and therefore no global coherence, and no global coordination in response to catastrophic and existential risk, which means, put simply, there will be, quite literally, no future.

HEALING THE GLOBAL INTIMACY DISORDER REQUIRES THE EVOLUTION OF INTIMACY

But we are not hopeless. On the contrary, we are filled with great hope. Hope is a memory of the future. That memory of the future *is* the direct hit that takes down the Death Star, the culture of death. **The direct hit must be**—as it has always been in history—**the emergence of a new stage of evolution**.

Crisis is an evolutionary driver, and every crisis is, at its core, a crisis of intimacy: from the oxygen crisis of the single cells dying which generated multicellular life at the dawn of existence, to the existential risk in this very moment.[9]

THE DIRECT HIT IS THEREFORE STRUCTURALLY SELF-EVIDENT: THE EVOLUTION OF INTIMACY ITSELF

What is intimacy, as a structure of Cosmos all the way down and all the way up the evolutionary chain? We engage this inquiry in depth in other writings, but for now we will simply adduce what we have called the "Intimacy Equation":

> Intimacy = shared identity in the context of [relative] otherness × mutuality of recognition × mutuality of pathos × mutuality of value × mutuality of purpose

Intimacy is about the capacity of parts to generate a *shared identity* while retaining their otherness, or distinct identity. This requires multiple mutualities, including recognition, pathos (or feeling), value, and purpose. The parts must recognize and feel each other, even as they share value and

---

9 We demonstrate this principle in some depth in the multi-volume series, *The Universe: A Love Story* (forthcoming) (https://worldphilosophyandreligion.org/early-ontologies), *The Intimate Universe: Global Intimacy Disorder as Cause for Global Action Paralysis* (forthcoming), and in other writings of CosmoErotic Humanism.

purpose. But all of this must lead to intimate union—and not pathological fusion, where the distinct identity of the parts disappears—like subatomic particles that successfully become an atom, or two people who successfully become a couple.

THE DECONSTRUCTION OF VALUE IS THE DECONSTRUCTION OF INTIMACY

We have identified the global intimacy disorder as the root cause of existential risk. But the underlying ultimate failure of intimacy is the deconstruction of value itself.

The deconstruction of value means that human value does not participate in any sense of intrinsic value of the Real. This is not about individual *values,* but about *the Field of Value* that underlies all of them. **When the human being**—moved, often sincerely or even nobly, by myriad cultural, historical, and psychological confusions—**claims to have stepped out of the Field of Value, then intimacy itself is deconstructed.**

The deconstruction of value is the deconstruction of intimacy.

In the absence of a shared Story of Value, a story that is an authentic expression of Reality's Eros, a story rooted in *pseudo-Eros* takes center stage and becomes the generator function for existential risk. Our modern pseudo-Eros story is *rivalrous conflict governed by win/lose metrics.* Such a story catalyzes in its wake the second generator function of existential risk: *complicated fragile systems with no allurement or intimacy between the parts.* It is in that sense that we have argued that the first generator function for existential risk is the success story.

- The failure of intimacy is precisely the impotent experience that there is no shared identity between the interior of the human being and Reality. **There is no shared identity in the sense of any kind of common participation in a field of shared intrinsic value.**

- **But only a shared Story of Value can arouse the global will required to engage catastrophic and existential risk.** For it is only global political, moral, and social will—and we can even say *erotic* will—that can generate the most Good, True and Beautiful world that we have always known is possible.

THE EVOLUTION OF LOVE IS THE TELLING OF A NEW STORY

Coupled with the Intimacy Equation is the scientifically grounded realization, in both the exterior and interior sciences, that Reality is a progressive deepening of intimacies, or, said slightly differently:

Reality is Evolution. Evolution is the evolution of intimacy.

- The evolution of intimacy requires—both personally and collectively—a deeper, more accurate discernment of the nature of our universe, ourselves, and our beloveds.
- This new discernment generates a new global Story of Value.
- The new global Story of Value generates an emergent, heretofore unseen global intimacy and heals the global intimacy disorder.

The new Story of Value is the direct hit that takes down the Death Star and replaces it with the hope that invokes the memory of our best future.

Global intimacy facilitates global coherence, which facilitates global coordination, which activates the possibility of our creative and effectively coordinated global responses to the global meta-crisis in its entirety and its specific expressions.

To solve Bertrand Russell's challenge—the apparent argument for the subjectivity of ethical values—**we have to reground value theory in eternal yet evolving First Principles and First Values, and articulate a new Story of Value.**

This is what we call CosmoErotic Humanism.

CosmoErotic Humanism—together with other emergent strands—**needs to become the ground of a world religion as a context for our diversity**. We need religion, even as we need science, to articulate a shared global grammar of value.

As we said at the beginning, our choice is simple: love or die.

- To love means to participate in the evolution of love, which is the evolution of the human Story of Value.
- To love means to evolve and activate a new cultural enlightenment—rooted in a new narrative of identity, a new narrative of value, a new narrative of intimate communion, a new narrative of desire, a new narrative of power—all of which will birth new narratives of economics and politics.
- The evolution of love is the telling of a new Story.

The new Story that must be told is a love story, for in fact that is the deepest truth of Reality, rooted in the best exterior and interior sciences, that we have at this moment in time:

- Reality is not merely a fact. Reality is a story.
- Reality is not an ordinary story. Reality is a love story.
- Reality is not an ordinary love story. Reality is an Outrageous Love Story.

Story doesn't mean it's *made-up*.

It means doing the hard work of integrating the validated insights of the traditional world, the modern world, and the postmodern world.

This is the intention at the heart of telling the new Story of CosmoErotic Humanism.

ABOUT THIS VOLUME

The book you are holding covers the key scenes and unspoken messages of two blockbuster movies released in theaters worldwide in the summer of 2023, *Barbie* and *Oppenheimer*.

The focus is particularly on the movie *Barbie*, a retelling of the "Barbie and Ken" girlfriend/boyfriend story especially familiar to young girls for decades.

One might guess that a movie about two plastic dolls is insignificant. But it is not.

At the cultural level, the movie's impact is dramatic, particularly since it was heralded as an icon of feminism by many reviewers and drew excited audiences among millions of young girls and their mothers.

But its "new" portrayal of relationship is utterly empty for all genders.

That summer *Barbie* was closely linked to *Oppenheimer;* an act of marketing genius that soon became known as "Barbenheimer." It seemed an odd combination—a story about two popular dolls and a story about the atomic bomb. But in fact, the two films are closely linked. Both unwittingly depict the destructive splits in relationship—one between the masculine and the feminine and one within the atom—that place human life at risk today.

Barbie does not claim that the relationship between Barbie and this particular Ken did not work out. **The point of the movie is that there is no Barbie and Ken—meaning that there is no inherent love story in Cosmos.** The very notion of the love story framing the narrative arc of our personal lives, our political lives, or our cosmic lives is seen as absurd.

Nor is it a story about Barbie evolving to claim her depth, as Ken evolves to claim his depth—which could then potentiate the possibility of their future love story. Not at all. There is just one core point in the texts of the movie: "Barbie and Ken" is illusion. Barbie is just Barbie. And Ken, who wants a love story, is an agent of patriarchy. As Gafni points out, the movie places the very idea that Reality might be a love story in the mouth of patriarchy. Love, in the tragic perspective of the *Barbie* movie, is but a strategy for power from which a very peculiar brand of feminism will liberate us.

In this book Marc Gafni reads both movies as "texts of culture," meaning that each tells a story-beneath-the-story. That deeper story seems not to be one the filmmakers knew they were telling, but it comes through clearly. We see it because it is there, if we know to look.

Gafni calls the narrator of the deeper story the Goddess, who appears at moments that reveal the truth of Eros at play in the Universe. Eros is the quality of aliveness and radiance in relationship that drives a new Story of Value: a true story moving culture toward wholeness. The Goddess speaks for a great love story of lines and circles as essential structures of Reality— deeper than masculine and feminine—that appear in sexuality no less than in the Universe itself. As we say in CosmoErotic Humanism, "All of Reality is always longing, always allured, always kissing, and always making love. That is the very nature of the Amorous Cosmos, from subatomic particles all the way to the human." This deeper structure is at the heart of this book.

Both films have left many viewers with an unmistakable sense of emptiness. Their response is often, "Where else could we go from here? What do we need to do?" These are questions that humans need to ask themselves: what does relationship really mean, and as one of the key songs poignantly asks, "What Was I Made For?" In *Barbie* such questions carry a sense of futility and despair, but this is wrong. They are the right questions. Our response to them is about the much more hopeful story that is available to all of us. It is about The Universe: A Love Story.[10]

---

10 For a deeper dive, see the forthcoming six-volume series *The Universe: A Love Story* (2026)

Because these talks were collected over the course of several months they introduce and re-introduce scenes from the two films alongside key themes in CosmoErotic Humanism. A certain amount of repetition is necessary, but new context is added each time. For new readers the footnotes offer a deeper dive into the Story of Value—of what matters—that is reflected here. For those already familiar with The Universe: A Love Story, these talks provide a way to read popular culture with nuance and wisdom, creating a new path for our evolution.

These oral essays are edited talks delivered by Marc Gafni—in One Mountain, Many Paths, on a podcast with Aubrey Marcus, at the Eros Mystery School, and in private teaching sessions—in late 2023.

Follow the link below to access the original material on which this book is based.

CHAPTER 1

READING MOVIES AS A SACRED TEXT OF CULTURE

STEPPING INTO CULTURE IN A REALLY SHOCKING WAY

One of the core practices in *CosmoErotic Humanism*,[11] the new Story of Value, is reading movies as sacred texts of public culture. One of the foils we are using to tell the new Story of Value is **exploring the way culture tells stories through movies.** In order to tell the new Story of Value, we need to tell it in response to the implicit stories that are being told today in culture.

We are engaging in the spiritual/political practice of reading a text of culture.

Reading texts of culture is critical. We can actually understand both where culture is and to what it is aspiring.

---

11 *CosmoErotic Humanism* is a world philosophical movement aimed at reconstructing the collapse of value at the core of global culture, which we are also referring to as the new Story of Value. Gafni will deepen our understanding of this in the course of this book.

Movies are prisoners to the most degraded and corrupt structures of culture—which are a kind of mass consumerism often speaking to the lowest common denominator of the human being—**and movies are also aspirational art forms that articulate visions of utopian possibility**, visions of the most noble, the most Good, the most True, the most Beautiful.

We've done very deep dives studying movies like *Dune, Avatar, Don't Look Up, Lord of the Rings*, and *Guardians of the Galaxy* with great attention, revealing the profound messages embedded within these films and asking:

- Is it an evolutionary story?
- Is it an important story?
- What's right about the story?
- What's wrong about the story?
- What does the movie tell us and not tell us about facing existential risk?

In the summer of 2023, two major films dominated the cultural landscape:

- *Oppenheimer*—a portrayal of Robert Oppenheimer, the father of the atomic bomb, who conceived the Los Alamos project.
- *Barbie*—a film that shattered box office records and captivated the world.

These movies didn't just succeed commercially—they resonated on a much deeper level.

So in this book, we will take a look at *Barbie* and *Oppenheimer* together in order to articulate—more sharply, more clearly—the new Story of Value.

But this book is also **a mini-course on how to read texts of culture** (which is not available anywhere else).

- How are each of the two movies an expression of the meta-crisis?
- Who are its key figures?
- What are its great love stories?

- What is the story beneath the story?
- What is the hidden narrative?
- What's the subtle play that is so easily missed when we look only at the surface?

At this moment *poised between utopia and dystopia*, let's dive into this deep heartthrobbing, ecstatic, urgent practice of participating in the evolution of culture and consciousness, which is the evolution of love.

THE GODDESS IS SPEAKING BEYOND THE INTENTION OF THE FILMMAKERS

In this book, we will show how *Barbie* and *Oppenheimer* are deeply related and how they are related to a much deeper issue, which is always *Eros*.

It is always the Goddess.

It is always *She*.

It is always the *Field of Desire*.

This conversation will really open up a whole new way of understanding movies.

We are not actually interested in the movies themselves. We are interested in what comes through them.

- We are interested in understanding what we are calling The Universe: A Love Story.
- We are interested in understanding *Eros*.
- We are interested in understanding what *the new human and the new humanity* is.

We read about 20 reviews of *Barbie* and 20 reviews of *Oppenheimer*, and they are all, tragically, an expression of the superficiality of culture. They are just jokes. I apologize for being so harsh, but they are so superficial, and so pathetic, and so tragic.

I am saying that this book is the right reading of *Oppenheimer* and *Barbie*, but I am *not* saying that this was *the conscious intention* of the filmmakers. A movie becomes a text of public culture, which is a Goddess text. **This is Eros speaking**. It doesn't matter what the filmmakers were thinking.

In other words, **there is a power to the movie, which is way beyond the conscious intention of the filmmakers**.

As I have shared with some of you before, when I spent a night with Lana Wachowski (who made *The Matrix* and *V for Vendetta*) and her partner, Karen, in Chicago, and we were reading the *V for Vendetta* and *The Matrix* movie, I said to Lana: "I don't care what you think about the movie, and the fact that you made it is very nice, but that doesn't give you more authority than me. In other words, the fact that you made the movie doesn't mean you're right about what it means. It just means you know what your intention is. You don't know what the movie is saying, you can't make that claim."

And she said, "That's absolutely true." She completely got that.

Both *Barbie* and *Oppenheimer* are actually great movies. *Oppenheimer* is particularly great, but *Barbie* is a great movie in its tragedy. It's reaching for something. There is a desperation in it. It comes out completely empty, but it captures—unintentionally—precisely what culture is.

In order for us to become *Homo amor*,[12] the fulfilment of *Homo sapiens*, we need to begin to learn how to read the texts of culture, because these are actually sacred texts of culture. They are *unintentional* sacred texts, so we need to know how to read them.

---

12 *Homo amor* is the term used in *CosmoErotic Humanism* for the new human. See *First Principles & First Values* (2024: Temple, David J. p.201-203): 'From Homo sapiens to Homo amor: the New Human and the New Humanity'

A HINT OF GUARDIANS OF THE GALAXY

We recommend seeing the movies *Barbie* and *Oppenheimer*. But if you can, also see all three parts of *Guardians of the Galaxy*. The *Guardians of the Galaxy* are incredibly important movies.

My friend Aubrey Marcus called and said, "What is this *Guardians of the Galaxy* really about?" He said, "What can you say about *Guardians of the Galaxy*?" On Aubrey's invitation, I did a deep dive into *Guardians of the Galaxy* for three nights, all night, and I watched them and wrote to myself, maybe 60 or 70 pages, analyzing the scenes in *Guardians of the Galaxy*—you can find this reading on Aubrey's podcast channel.

Now, why did I know that it would work? I knew it would work for a simple reason. *Guardians of the Galaxy* swept a certain part of culture. It swept people who were 20 to 50 years old, something like that. The senior boomers didn't get it, but Aubrey's whole crowd loved it. This whole world loved *Guardians of the Galaxy*—and I knew if everyone loved it, there must be something happening there that's real. It turns out that it's fascinating.

But of course, none of the reviews get it. You have to go deeper. When I say *none of the reviews get it*, I don't mean that in an arrogant way. It's just true. You be the judge after you've listened to the podcast we did on *Guardians*, whether we got it at a whole different level or not. But it's not because we are smart. It's not about being smart, that's not the point. The point is, **you have to feel *into the inside***, you have to treat every dialogue with respect, and notice that even though it's not the intention of the filmmaker, it is what *actually happens*.

I am just going to give you one hint. *Guardians of the Galaxy* completely changes our relationship to trauma. It changes our relationship to Unique Self.[13] It changes our relationship to love, to Eros. Everything changes. It's

---

13 The Unique Self narrative of identity integrates the crucial insights of all the great wisdom traditions, East and West, into a powerful, profound, and accurate response to the great inquiry of Who Am I? See *Your Unique Self: the Radical Path to Personal Enlightenment* (2012).

unbelievably important, this silly movie, which has a raccoon as one of its stars. Rocket the Raccoon is one of the stars, and Rocket the Raccoon turns out to be very serious.

If you really want to do it seriously, if you want to really challenge yourself to *read culture...*it sounds like it's easy. But it actually takes enormous energy and commitment to do anything well. If you watch *Guardians of the Galaxy,* you have to watch all three and **trace the development of the characters through the three movies**.

If you can read these texts, you can actually become *Homo amor*. In other words, **by knowing how to read these texts, and beginning to develop the eyes of love that can look at culture and understand the play, we can move to transform culture.**

Because everything happening in *Guardians* is happening *in me.* That's the thing. It is all happening in me. If I cannot read it in *Guardians*, I cannot read it in me.

I can go to a therapist from today til whenever. Believe me, the therapists are the people who are reading *Barbie* exactly in that limited way. It's a therapeutic culture that created *Barbie.* It's tragic.

So, being able to read *Barbie* is not a cute assignment. It's a deep insight practice, to be able to read the text of culture.

Aubrey and I also did a deep dive reading on *Lord of the Rings* and on *Barbie* (which you can find both on his podcast and in chapter 12 of this book).

BARBIE: THE MOST DANGEROUS MOVIE EVER MADE

In this book we will focus first on the movie *Barbie*, and in *Barbie* we are going to take a look at two stories.

- One is a story that culture made up, *Barbie. Barbie* is a story. It's a story about Barbie, and about Barbie and Ken. It's a story incarnated in a doll.

- And then, *Barbie* as a movie, which is a story about the story.

Culture told a story about *Barbie*. The movie *Barbie* broke box office records all over the place, so it resonated all over the world. People are watching it all over the world. It is entering into the heart stream and the bloodstream of culture.

Barbie is one of the highest grossing movies in the world now. It's in the top, I think, twenty-five of all time. It is a very fascinating movie, but again, the reviews on *Barbie* don't have *the slightest clue* what it's actually about.

This movie has entered culture, and the Barbie doll is in culture. Barbie is the doll that women have grown up with and played with for generations, around the world. The movie is a very subtle movie that gets it exactly half right and exactly half wrong.

We are going to look at that story, and we are going to see:

- How does that story relate to an accurate story of Reality?
- What is the story that's being told in culture now?

We are going to use that as a mirror to get us to a deeper story, to a more profound story, which will blow our hearts open.

As we are going to see, ***Barbie* is, I would say, the most dangerous movie ever made (or at least recently).**

Seriously, the most dangerous movie ever made.

Not dangerous in a good way—as when Lao Tzu, the great Chinese sage says: *I come to speak dangerous words, I ask only that you listen dangerously* (that's my favorite citation). But no, *Barbie* does not speak those kinds of dangerous words. They are dangerous words:

- which are *insidious*,
- which *undermine* the joy of Reality,
- which are empirically not valid, but *pretend to be valid*,

- that have hosts of *hidden assumptions* which are actually dogmatic, and which are setting the agenda of culture.

The story of culture is told in movies—it's the story that culture makes up around itself, in its cinematic form, and tells around the campfire of celluloid.

Around this celluloid campfire, we tell our stories, and it's those stories that define culture.

THE POINT OF *BARBIE* IS THAT LOVE IS NOT REAL

The starting point of the movie *Barbie* is the triumph of second-wave feminism, the liberation of the feminine from the constricting social roles of the past. But it is marred by Barbie's complete alienation from the truth of The Universe: A Love Story.

The great mystic Isaac Luria said, "Reality is lines and circles, all the way up and all the way down." And lines and circles live in me. That's my love story. When I am CosmoErotic Humanism in person, then I can engage the next love story. I can be a mad lover on all the levels.

So when I say *a line and a circle,* I don't mean men and women. I mean that in the core structure of Reality, there is *a line* and *a circle.* There is a line quality and a circle quality in the core structure of Cosmos. There is this deep allurement between the line and the circle.

That's the core of Cosmos.

This is the dance of allurement, which is Cosmos itself. Reality is Eros all the way up and all the way down. The quality of Eros is desire, and it is the desire for greater intimacy.

Intimacy means more wholeness in the context of shared identities and [relative] otherness.

Evolution is the progressive deepening of intimacies.

Evolution is a story of clarifying allurements. My Unique Self is my unique set of allurements. And there's always the dance between line and circle.

There is this sense of, *Wow! I begin to appear in a new way in your gaze*, which is the essence of what a love story is. *When you look at me, something new emerges in me, I begin to live in a new way and some deeper part of me emerges in your gaze, and the relationship between us is not just a social construction.*

Now, along comes modernity and says, "No, value is not quite real." Modernity doesn't say it out loud. David Hume, if you read him carefully, was quite clear about it, but it's hidden because that was too radical a thing to say.

For example, in the American Constitution, we say, "We hold these truths to be self-evident," which is another way of saying, "We have no idea where these things are from, but this is how we're going to live." That's what *self-evident* means here. We can't *source* these values. They're not sourced in revelation, but we are going to live in them. **We deconstruct the Field of Value, but we live in it anyways.**

But the one value that still lives at the center is love. Another way of saying this is:

We killed all the Gods except for Aphrodite, the Goddess of love.

When the World Trade Center was about to come down, what most people did was call one person to say, "I love you." Aphrodite is still somehow there.

9

Somehow, even after we deconstructed all the values, we still assume that love is real.

When we go to *ChatGPT,* the oracular structure of a new emergent AI, and we ask, "Is love real?" It says, *not quite.* And there is this seeping influence that has existed in literature, and all over the place, which deconstructs value and deconstructs love with it.

But popular culture still insisted love is real—until *Barbie.*

You get what a big deal that is?

The point of the *Barbie* movie is that there is no Field of Value, there is no Ken and Barbie, love is not real, and Reality is not a love story.

The assumption we make is that love is always going to be real. But look at *ChatGPT* together with *Barbie*—you begin to see where we're going. We're going very fast off a cliff, where there is no Field of Value.

A NEW WORLD ORDER

I was visiting Bretton Woods[14] in New Hampshire the other day. Bretton Woods intended to create a new world order, but it ultimately failed. It lasted till maybe 1972 when Nixon unhooked the dollar from certain standards, and the whole *Pax Americana*[15] that kept the world together for forty to fifty years is now falling apart.

In other words, the New World Order established after World War II has actually collapsed. The Bretton Woods order has collapsed.

We're here to create a new world order. We are here to create a new world. We've come back to Bretton Woods to get it right.

---

14 Bretton Woods was the site of the United Nations Monetary and Financial Conference in 1944 which has given its name to the Bretton Woods system and led to the establishment of both the World Bank and the International Monetary Fund in 1945.

15 The concept of relative peace in the Western Hemisphere after the end of World War II in 1945.

We need to be able to become the new human. We need to move from *Homo sapiens* to *Homo amor—the new human and the new humanity.*

We need to be able to do sensemaking, and sensemaking is the ability to make sense of Cosmos, because Cosmos lives in me.

- I can only do that if I know how to read the texts of my own interiors and if I know how to read texts of culture.
- I can only do that if I have a Story of Value—the First Principles and First Values that allow me to make sense of what's happening around us.

We are in a time between worlds and a time between stories. **We are reading texts of culture in order to evolve the very source code of culture,** which I believe—based on everything I know, having worked on this 18 hours a day for the last 20 years—is the only way to respond to the meta-crisis. And the alternative is suffering of unimaginable dimensions for generations.

If we actually understand that the meta-crisis is real, and that the response to the meta-crisis has to be a new Story of Value out of which we generate a new Reality, then we have to go look at those stories of cultures. **We need to know how to *read* these stories.** This is why we are going to look at this story of *Barbie*. We are going to look at it slowly, one step at a time.

CHAPTER 2

THE GENDER CRISIS IS PART OF THE META-CRISIS

THREE CRISES HAPPENING AT THE SAME TIME

A meta-crisis means that:

- There are cascading risks in various sectors that interplay with each other.
- At its very core, two systems—the civilization and the substrate of the biosphere and physiosphere—are clashing with each other in such a way that the civilization may essentially self-terminate, resulting in the death of humanity.

The energy substrates, the resource substrates, and the systems upon which it is all built have crossed the planetary boundaries. They are now exceedingly fragile, and are subject to imminent collapse. Whether *imminent* means 10, 20, 30, or 40 years, is an open question, but **there is a serious and significant possibility that the entire thing could collapse.** That's called the meta-crisis.

There is a second form of the meta-crisis, which is not the death of humanity, but the potential death of *our* humanity. This can happen because **we respond to the fragile global systems animated by exponential technologies by *closing up* society**. This occurs either in an obvious totalitarian way, with an obvious closed society, or through **an *invisible* closed society**. In that case we don't realize it's closed, but it begins to be guided by a system in which:

- everyone is a number,
- everyone's opinions are controlled,
- the feeds that we see are controlled,
- how we respond to those feeds—at least enough of a percentage of us—is invisibly controlled, and
- every election and every decision is made by the way we optimize the web and the way we optimize new forms of invisible control.

That's what we call the death of *our* humanity.

The gender crisis is one crucial aspect of the meta-crisis, although the gender crisis completely ignores the meta-crisis. In *Barbie* it is as if there is no meta-crisis, as if existential risk is not real. The movie is lost in its own pathos. But *Barbie* is actually deeply related to the meta-crisis, because the core point of the movie is that there is no intrinsic love story between the sexes, or between genders. In other words, there is no "Barbie and Ken."

- So first, let's notice that **the meta-crisis is happening at the same time as the gender crisis.** The meta-crisis that's happening around the world is happening *at the exact same time* where we have this massive crisis questioning what it means to be a man or a woman, or what *is* a man, and what *is* a woman. The complexity and confusion around that issue is enormous. In many ways, *Barbie* is about this gender crisis. In its own self-understanding, it's about **what it means to be a man or a woman.** I would call it a *gender identity crisis*. That's one.

- Two, there is a crisis of *sexuality*: we don't have a sexual story, we don't have a sexual narrative. We have *a crisis of desire.*
- Three, there is an actual meta-crisis of *existential risk,* in which we risk the death of humanity—or, through various forms of what we call *TechnoFeudalism,*[16] we risk turning Reality into a kind of *Skinner box* (a box in which rats and pigeons are controlled by the controllers of the box, even though they're unaware that they are being controlled). There are two kinds of existential risks: the death of humanity, and the death of *our* humanity.[17]

There are no coincidences in the Intimate Universe.

The fact that the gender crisis and the crisis of desire are happening at the exact same time as the meta-crisis is significant.

Both the movie *Barbie* and the movie *Oppenheimer,* which released at the same time, speak directly into this. We will get to *Oppenheimer* in chapter eleven.

THERE IS NO BARBIE AND KEN

The message behind *Barbie* as a cultural text is that Reality is *not* a love story. Any Eros and allurement that exists between Barbie and Ken is a mere social construction. It is not an expression of the essential nature of Cosmos itself—or what we have variously called the CosmoErotic Universe, The Universe: A Love Story, or the Intimate Universe.

---

16 TechnoFeudalism means that the vast majority of humanity will be enclosed, like Skinner's experimental rats and pigeons, in a Skinner box, subject to "invisible" "techniques of control," which are constantly—and again, "invisibly"—"shaping," "controlling," "manipulating," "conditioning," "engineering," and "tuning" human behavior for ends established by the hidden "planners" and "controllers." See *Invisible Architects: Skinner, Pentland & the Hidden Blueprints for Technofeudalism. Exit the Silicon Maze. Vol. 2* (2025, Temple, David J.)

17 For a deeper understanding of these two forms of existential risk, see *First Principles & First Values* (2024: Temple, David J. p 39-44

In this sense, responding to *Barbie* is the same as responding to the meta-crisis. What's the basic point of *Barbie* from the perspective of Barbie and Ken? It's that "Barbie and Ken" as a love story doesn't exist.

Early in *Barbie*, Ken tries to kiss Barbie, but she backs away. When he asks if he can spend the night, she says "It's girls' night, all night, every night, forever." In other words, there is no "Barbie and Ken." They are a myth. **Not only is Barbie not in love with Ken, but the very ontological notion of "Barbie and Ken" is rendered absurd by the movie.**

The notion of the love story is represented by Ken, in the moments in the movie when he wants to spend the night with Barbie and share a house with her. But he's clearly revealed to be a failure, a pathetic expression of patriarchy. So his attempts at telling a love story are seen as a failure as well.

Only if love is a value, a First Principle and First Value of Cosmos, is there a reason to connect, to make love, to be aroused. But there is no intimacy, no Eros, no arousal between Barbie and Ken. In fact, the notion that there would be "Barbie and Ken" in the movie seems almost offensive.

In a telling scene later in the movie, Barbie declares that she doesn't love Ken. She's not referring to a particular Ken, not the Ken that the actor Ryan Gosling plays. No, *all* **the men in the movie are named Ken**, so she means that she doesn't love *any* Ken. Barbie's love for any of them is impossible.

In another scene, she says to him that he has to become Ken, but she does not mean in order to come back to union with Barbie from a higher place. There is no higher place. The point of Barbie is not for Ken to individuate and come back to form a higher union with Barbie. There can be no love story because there is no Field of Value in the movie, nor in culture at large. There is no sense of Eros = Value, no sense of *Eros Value*. As we unpack in *CosmoErotic Humanism,* the words Eros and Value come together because there is no split between them.[18]

---

18 See *First Principles & First Values* (2024: p 177-179)

WE THINK WE CAN KILL ALL THE GODS EXCEPT FOR APHRODITE AND SHE WILL SURVIVE, BUT SHE WILL NOT

In every relationship—whether it's two guys, two girls, a romance or a friendship, whether it's an organization, whether it's a company—in order to create coherence and resonance, or actual intimacy, you need a shared Field of Value. If you don't have this shared Field of Value, you cannot create intimacy or coherence or resonance or depth—it can't be done. You need some minimal shared value. The more shared value you have, the deeper intimacy you have. But minimally, there has to be a ground of shared value.

This is what Ken and Barbie are missing.

We think we can kill all of the gods except Aphrodite, and that she will survive. But Aphrodite—the Goddess of love—will not survive on her own. No matter how much we praise love in our culture, Aphrodite is only nourished from the Field of Value. **If you cut a flower at its root, it takes a few days, but ultimately it dies.** Similarly, if you cut love from the Field of Eros Value, it too withers and dies.

So, we have this huge, gorgeous *Barbie* movie that's being seen around the world, a huge blockbuster. It's become this major statement of culture, a drama being written about every place, getting an enormous amount of attention. **And the basic point of the movie is that there is no love story possible.** It's an important text of culture, both in what it gets and what it doesn't get.

In the old world of cinema, as well as the old world of literature, which was also our old psychological world, it was a given that it's always a love story, and that Reality itself is in some sense a love story.

The entire point of *Barbie* is that it's not a love story. It's about the absurd notion that there even *would* be a love story at the center. In this worldview without a love story at the center, there is no Barbie and Ken— there simply can't be.

16

RESPONDING TO THE META-CRISIS WITH A NEW STORY OF VALUE

We are here to invoke the dawn of a new narrative of desire, which is **a new narrative of what it means to be a human being**—because desire is the desire for new value.

- Desire desires *value*, and we live in a Field of Value.
- That Field of Value is also a Field of Eros. Eros and value are one, and there is no split between them.
- Reality is ErosValue, all the way down and all the way up the evolutionary chain.

Our context is that, actually, there is good news.

Gospel means "good news." There *is* a new gospel; there *is* good news—but it comes not from the revelation of just one person. **It comes from the deepest read that we have of the interior sciences and the exterior sciences, and their coming together in a new *superstructure*.**[19]

A new superstructure means:

- a new set of **worldviews,**
- a new set of **dreams,**
- a new set of **values,**
- and a new Story of Value rooted in First Principles and First Values.

We are here to be extremely pragmatic and filled with wild celebration.

We are celebrating because we can only change the world if we are willing to already live in the world that's already changed.

---

19 We distinguish between superstructure (the set of worldviews, grammars, ideas, philosophies, realizations, stories, wisdom, principles, and values that animate a society), social structure (the agreements, legal systems, contracts, business models, and governance structures of society), and infrastructure (the physical built environments and technologies that provide for the material needs required by the social structure and superstructure). See *First Principles and First Values* (2024), 26.

We have to change the world, not from a place of resignation, not from a place of depression, but **from the direct experience of the joy of Reality.**

Accessing the full aliveness of Reality, moving in me, as me, and through me.

Accessing the full Eros of Reality, moving in me, as me, and through me.

Accessing the full desire of Reality, living in me, as me, and through me.

Because Reality is desire. Reality is Eros. Reality is value.

There is a Field of Value that reaches for new possibility. A Field of Value generates a new world and a new vision, and this new vision generates a new Story of Value, from within which we create.

We are here to respond to the meta-crisis—like da Vinci and his cohorts did in the Renaissance—by enacting a new Story of Value, rooted in First Principles and First Values, a universal grammar of value as a context for our diversity.

That's what we are doing.

We can't go to *the Doomer, the Denial, or the Dominator*[20] vision of Reality. Those are devastating. **What we need is a new *Dawn of Desire.***

A new Dawn of Desire means a new Story of Value, which answers three questions:

- Where are we?

---

20 The three classical responses to the meta-crisis—doomer, denial, domination—won't work. The fourth response—the only way to cross to the other side—is *the dawn of desire*: the *clarified* desire for more *value*, for the future that is not yet here. See *One Mountain, Many Paths*, episode 362—*The Response to the Meta-Crisis Is the Dawn of Desire* in *Codes of Desire: On the Nature of Reality—The Answer to Where, Who and What* (Gafni, 2024). Published here: https://worldphilosophyreligion.substack.com/p/362-the-response-to-the-meta-crisis.

- Who are we?
- What ought we be doing?

Those are the three great questions of *CosmoErotic Humanism* that are at the core of a new Story of Value. A new Story of Value means a new story of desire, because desire implies value, and clarified desire equals value.

CHAPTER 3

CRISIS OF RELATIONSHIPS

In the previous chapter, we noted that three crises are happening simultaneously: the gender crisis, a crisis of desire, and the meta-crisis. These three are significantly related. In this context, we can deepen our understanding of the gender crisis. We can explore how the gender crisis generates a crisis of relationship, by looking at three levels of gender and how they relate to three levels of relationship.

THE FIRST TWO LEVELS OF GENDER

Feminine and Masculine, Level-One:
He Is In Charge

First, I just want to put a framework in place. We're going to talk about three levels of relationship to our own *feminine* or *masculine,* to our own inner man or woman.

For now, I'm going to use the words *man* and *woman* synonymously with *masculine* and *feminine.*

I am obviously deeply aware of the fact that men are both feminine and masculine, and women are both feminine and masculine. There is a lot to say about that, and we have done a huge dive at Eros Mystery School[21] into the new human and the new gender, and what that means.[22] We have critiqued gender ideology (the leveling of differences between men and women) and the old gender view. We have begun to create, for the first time, a new view of gender. **We have begun to articulate *Homo amor*'s view of gender.**

So we have done a deep dive into this topic at the Mystery School, but for now, I just want to use *masculine* and *feminine,* and *man* and *woman* together. I am not going to make the distinction, to make it easy for our conversation.

Let's see if we can do this.

Let's call it *level-one woman* and *level-one man.*

Level-one woman is the classical feminine. I want to identify "level-one woman" as the classical woman of, let's say, the fifties in the United States or in Europe—before feminism.

- **Her job is to be somebody's wife and somebody's mother.** It's not enough to be somebody's daughter. She has to be somebody's wife or mother, she has to take care of them.
- She has to **look beautiful** *all the time,* because that's what she's supposed to do.
- She's supposed to **never lose her cool.**
- Her job is to be the perfect woman.
- **She needs to be recognized by a man.** If she's not recognized by a man, she's not doing it right.

---

21 Eros Mystery School is a yearly intensive in Europe, see erosmysteryschool.com.
22 See: *From Gender Crisis to Unique Gender: The Erotic Cosmos of Lines, Circles, and Spirals. Hieros Gamos and Evolutionary Relationships* (Gafni, 2025)

That's the job of the feminine. I am not taking the time to give a full description, obviously. But this is level one: the job of the feminine is to seduce the man, to get a husband, in order to have a relationship, in order to have stability and security, in order to have children, in order to raise the next generation, or whatever it might be.

The level-one man is, of course, the classical fifties man.

- He has to be **a protector and a provider**, and he is the person **in charge**—it is **classical patriarchy** in all of those senses.
- He needs to have a wife, and although he clearly is moved by the feminine, in the end, he is in charge.
- He is making the rules.
- He is being the doctor, and he's the lawyer, and he's winning the Nobel Prize, and he's the politician—and she is in a support role.

How does sexuality work between them?

Sexuality between a level-one man and level-one-woman is, fundamentally, he is in charge.

In classical level-one, we didn't even have any laws against sexual harassment, they didn't even exist. I mean, it's so dramatic that in many states in the United States and countries in Europe, *marital rape*—being raped by your husband—wasn't even on the books. It was not even illegal, it didn't even exist. You were supposed to submit to your man. No one had written anything about the G-spot. My dear friend, her mother actually wrote the book, *The G-Spot*. She just passed at 102. She was a student of Reich's. But this is *before* that, we are at level one. This is before *The G-Spot* was written. It's before feminine orgasm actually had a place in the modern world.

Let me be clear, in the ancient world, it was much different. I am not talking about *all* of history. I am talking about the classic vision of the last hundred years.

Feminine and Masculine, Level-Two: The Disappearance of Polarity

Level-two woman and level-two man, as we are going to see, is where the movie *Barbie* happens. In level two, it's not about the man who is in charge, and the woman who supports. It's egalitarian.

- The man has become more sensitive and more kind, and he is reading a little Rumi, and he is more of a sensitive New Age guy, and he is a little more in touch with his feelings—just a little bit.
- The woman has a job, and she got into medical school, and she got into law school, and she's winning some Nobel Prizes.

There is more equality between men and women, and men and women are partners now. **That's the ideal *role*, they are partners.**

But at this level, it also gets a little complicated. This is where *Barbie* is going to start, and it gets complicated for a couple of reasons.

First, sexuality starts to disappear.

I am going to say something very wild and funny, and not so funny. In most classical liberal households around the world, in most marriages, there is almost no sex at all. That's just true. No one says it out loud, but basically, there is not much sex happening in marriages all over the liberal world. That's just true.

Now, *why?*

It's for a bunch of reasons. One is, **there is no story of desire; there is no sexual narrative.** But that's not our topic now.

There is another reason, which is that **there is no polarity.** There is this equal partnership, and everyone is working really hard at being equal. But **there is no polarity, and this means there is not the play of magnets.** When you have these two roles—he is the provider, and she is the homemaker—there is this *polar balance between them*. There is *attraction* or *allurement,* and then there is also *autonomy*. When you have these very different defined roles, there is what's called polarity.

In the modern egalitarian couple, they are either both working, or *only she* is working. As we will see, this is also going to be key to the movie *Barbie*.

A very important book, written in 2011, which conquered the American markets, is called *The End of Men and the Rise of Women*, written by an Israeli woman, Hanna Rosin, who is a classical Western liberal. She writes for *Slate*. It's basically about men not having a job. It is about manufacturing jobs ending around the world and women becoming more and more the primary breadwinners. We're are about to cross the 50% line, where most homes actually have a woman as a primary breadwinner, not a man.

Wow! The woman doesn't have to be a homemaker anymore. Contraception has created a split between children and sexuality. Women are working, they are getting jobs, they are employed—and women began to ask the question, *why do we need a man?*

- I can have sex when I want to, if I want to.
- I don't need a man in order to survive, in order to make a living.
- The communication is not so good between us anyways, because he never understands what I am talking about, so why do I need a man?

That becomes the big question: why do I need a man?

The polarity is gone. The protector/homemaker is gone. Either we have an equal relationship, or we have the woman as the primary breadwinner. So where is the polarity? How does polarity happen?

Polarity has to happen in a new way. **Something new has to happen**. Unless that something new happens, unless there is a new relationship, unless there is a new *quality* of relationship, the polarity disappears—and with the polarity, sexuality disappears as well.

Isn't that amazing?

Sexuality disappears in a relationship by a combination of several things:

- First, **sexuality is available outside of the home**, so lots of people find ways to have sexuality outside of the home.
- Second, there is pornography, which changes the game. **Instantly available pornography changes reality**, not just on the male side, but on the female side too.
- Third, which is a very big deal, **the sense of *desire* to be sexing disappears**—because sexing was part of this larger relationship, this larger polarity, this larger wholeness.

Again, many men now don't have jobs, we have this huge class of men all over the Western world who have lost manufacturing jobs. They are not in the small 5% of the elite of lawyers and accountants and bankers and doctors—the overwhelming majority of men are not in that category. Many men are not being primary breadwinners, and women are saying, *I am not attracted*.

Just like men have often been attracted to the body of the woman, women have often been attracted to *the body of the car.* By the body of the car, I mean **the capacity of the man to be a protector**. Actually, many women objectify men, just like men objectify women. It works on both sides. **When we don't have men as the male protector, a lot of the objectification and the attraction actually disappears.**

So, that's level two.

At level two, it's not actually feminist and cool to be a sexy woman in the same old way.

- You are *not* supposed to be *seducing men.*
- You are supposed to have an *independent identity*, to be independent of men.

However, in this second stage, in this classical feminism, **becoming this new woman actually means becoming more like a man**. *I become more like a man*:

- I have a job.
- I am not doing the hot sexual thing anymore.
- I have to hide my emotions because I am supposed to be in the workplace. *And why am I getting all emotional anyway?*

Men don't know who they are, because there are millions and millions, tens of millions of men all over the world who aren't the protector anymore. They are not the people who are earning the money. **Unless I have a strong sense of identity from someplace else, then *who am I?***

That's our frame.

We did not get to level-three relationships yet. Let's first look at how these two levels of relationship play out in *Barbie*.

TWO LEVELS OF RELATIONSHIP APPLIED TO BARBIE

"It's Girls' Night Every Night Forever!"

With these first two levels of relationship in mind, we are going to look at *Barbie*.

Barbie opens with these perfect women. We are in Barbie Land. We are in the world of Barbie.

In this *Barbie* movie, there are two worlds. **There is the Barbie world and the real world.** This is shamanic and interesting. There is this very subtle connection between the real world and the Barbie world that takes place when a girl plays with her doll:

- If a girl plays with her doll in an ordinary way, the two worlds remain separate.

- But there are certain moments where the girl who's playing with the doll can get in a certain kind of mood, where that mood somehow enters the doll, and then enters the doll world, the Barbie world.

The worlds are supposed to be separate—but every once in a while, some travesty, some disaster, some catastrophe happens, and the worlds mix. That's what is happening in the movie.

The movie opens with the Barbie world, and all the women look perfect, and the star of the movie is named Barbie. She is the Stereotypical Barbie doll. All of her friends are perfect, with perfect makeup, perfect hair, and perfect bodies—but they are in a women's world. This is really important. They are in a women's world, and they say, *All the girls in the real world are really supportive of Barbie because Barbie has allowed them to be doctors, and lawyers, and Nobel Prize winners.*

The Barbie doll began as just a classical level-one woman. She seduces her man. She looks beautiful. That's how Barbie begins, but then the Mattel toy company up-levels Barbie, and Barbie begins to become all sorts of things. She becomes a doctor, and a lawyer, and a Nobel Prize winner. We are in Barbie Land, and all the Barbies are really proud of themselves because they say, *We are empowering women all over the world. We are showing them how to be doctors and lawyers and Nobel Prize winners.* That's Barbie.

Who is the girl? Barbie.

Who is the guy? Ken.

Ken has these perfectly ripped abs, just like me (No, I'm just kidding. That's not true. Only in my dreams.) So, Ken has this perfectly ripped body, he's gorgeous, and his shirt is, of course, always wide open. When we first meet Ken, the narrator says: "Barbie has a great day every day. Ken only has a great day when Ken looks at him." Ken only feels good if he is in Barbie's gaze, if Barbie looks at him.

Barbie herself has moved from level-one woman to level-two woman.
The movie doesn't say *level one* and *level two*, they don't use these words,
but she is first a classical 1950s girl, and then she moves to level two, where
she is powerful. We see seven or eight scenes of Barbie being awarded a
diploma, Barbie graduating from graduate school, Barbie becoming a
doctor, Barbie being a law professor. Barbie got to level two.

What does Ken do? Ken does not have a job. Ken is not a lifeguard, Ken
is not a lawyer, Ken is not a doctor. What does Ken do? Ken *beaches*. The
word *beach*, *beach* as a verb.

Ken "beaches," that's what he knows how to do.

Ken *beaches*—that's what Ken does.

Now, it looks cute in the movie—but when you begin to listen carefully, it's
actually pathetic and tragic.

Ken has no job. Barbie will look at Ken and she'll smile at Ken. There are
lots of Kens on the beach, and Barbie smiles at them, looks at them, and
waves at them. When Barbie looks at them, they feel great. But then Barbie
leaves, and Ken says, "Can I come to your house tonight?" Barbie says,
"Sure, because we are having a big girls' party." Ken comes to the house,
and Ken dances, all the different Kens are dancing, the men dance with the
women—but then the women throw them out. Barbie says, "It's girls' night
tonight, and it's girls' night every night forever!" Meaning, *we don't need
Ken.* Ken leans in, he is reaching for a kiss, he is reaching for sexuality—
and Barbie is like, *who are you?* She doesn't even know what sexuality is.
So she rejects him.

Later in the movie, when Barbie and Ken go to the real world, they have
a conversation with the construction crew, Barbie says to them: "I do not
have a vagina, and he does not have a penis. We don't have genitals."

What's the point? **The point is that there is no sexuality happening.** There
is no Eros there. We are at this level-two place, in which men don't have a

role, and women are doing *girls' night forever.* But the polarity is completely lost.

It's fascinating.

BARBIE STOPS AT LEVEL TWO: THERE IS NO BARBIE AND KEN

Now stay close, it gets even more interesting.

There is no love story at level-two Barbie. This is where culture is, this is the story that culture is telling.

There is no sense of polarity, there is no story around a *need* to be a man or a woman.

When I say *man/woman, man/man, woman/woman,* for the sake of this conversation, let's assume we're including all aspects of LGBTQ+ relationships, even though the *Barbie* movie, interestingly, didn't address them, and instead skipped it entirely. The *Barbie* movie focused only on man and woman, which was actually the bravest thing the whole movie did.

But basically, the movie stops at level two. There is no room for "Ken and Barbie," they don't even have genitals.

Now, what happens? It gets completely wild. We are going to do a deep cultural analysis, and it's gorgeous.

Barbie is at the party, and then in the middle of this incredible dance number at the party, she says, "Do you guys ever think about dying?"

The music stops.

Thinking about death?

Everyone stops like, *Oh my god, you're thinking about dying?* It ruins the whole thing, and then there's this uncomfortable silence—but then she says, "I am just dying to dance!" Everyone breathes a sigh of relief—*it's okay, we are dying to dance.*

The dancing goes on.

There's this weird thing, a malfunction: she's thinking about death, and she can't understand why.

Then, Barbie wakes up in the morning, and she is thinking about death again. Her breath isn't good in the morning—and remember, she is called the *Stereotypical Barbie.* The Stereotypical Barbie is always perfect—her hair is always perfect, she always looks great, she's always perfectly calm and perfectly fantastic. But she wakes up in the morning, and her breath is bad, she's thinking about death again, and her feet are flat (meaning, they don't go into high heels).

She goes to the beach and she says, "Oh my god, my feet are flat." The other Barbie dolls tell her, "If you have flat feet, you have to go to Weird Barbie." Weird Barbie is this one weird doll that was discontinued. "You have to go to Weird Barbie and talk to her." So Stereotypical Barbie knocks on the door of Weird Barbie, and Weird Barbie says, "Oh my god, you have flat feet!"

And then she picks up Barbie's skirt and she says, "Look, you have cellulite!" (meaning, your legs aren't exactly perfect, you have cellulite). And Barbie wails, "Oh my god, that's terrible, what am I going to do?"

Weird Barbie says to Stereotypical Barbie,

> "You've opened a portal. And now, there is a rip in the continuum that is the membrane between Barbie Land and the real world, and if you wanna be Stereotypical Barbie again, then, baby girl, you gotta go fix it. You have to go to the real world and find the girl who is playing with you. The girl who's playing with you, she must be sad, and her thoughts and feelings and humanness are interfering with your doll-ness."

Weird Barbie says that there must have been some connection made between Barbie and someone in the real world. That's what is going wrong. The only thing she can do to save herself is to go to the real world and break that connection, and if she breaks that connection, then her flat feet will be gone and her cellulite will be gone.

She doesn't want to go to the real world, but she has no choice.

She gets in her little Barbie car, and she starts moving towards the real world.

BARBIE RECLAIMS HER SEXUALITY WITHOUT KEN

She starts moving, moving, moving towards the real world. You have to take a car, and a boat, and a plane, and a submarine, and a helicopter. It's this long trip, a cartoon trip, but as she starts the trip, she sees Ken in the back seat. She's horrified. What is he doing there?

Ken has come with her because **Ken *loves her*.** You get this, friends? Ken does not have a job, but Ken loves her, and Ken doesn't even feel like a man if he is not in Barbie's gaze. But he can't say that, it can't be done.

They begin to move to the world of real people. They get to Venice Beach in Santa Monica in Los Angeles. They are wearing these Barbie clothes—Ken's wearing his Ken outfit, and Barbie is wearing her Barbie clothes. There are all these cool LA people, and they look at them like *you guys are completely crazy*, so they change their clothes.

And then they realize this is weird: no one is thanking them for being Barbie and Ken, people are looking at them like they're weird and crazy. They are a little devastated.

Then there is this construction crew I told you about. They start whistling at Barbie and making fun of them, and she goes over and says,

> "I am sensing an undertone of violence in that whistle. I don't know what you meant with all of those little quips, but I'm pick-

31

ing up some sort of entendre, which appears to be double, and I would just like to inform you, I do not have a vagina, and he does not have a penis. We don't have genitals."

And the construction crew looks at them like *who are you, you're crazy.*

Barbie and Ken go on their different journeys—each goes on an entirely different journey. I am not going to take you on the whole journey, but I want to jump to the end now.

What happens? And this is just a quick recapitulation of the ending, we'll get deeper into this in the rest of the book.

In the end, Barbie has to move *beyond* being Barbie, but she doesn't quite get there.

Barbie has to realize: *Oh, poor Ken, he doesn't have a job, he's just dependent on me.* She says to Ken, "Ken, you have to be willing to be Ken, just as Ken," which is great.

But it's very clear that **Barbie doesn't *need* Ken**. Ken embraces himself as being Ken, but he doesn't know what that means. He sings his song, "I'm just Ken," but Ken remains pathetic—he doesn't have a sense of what it means to be a man.

Barbie, in the very last scene in the movie, decides to stay in the real world, in real people's land.

The last thing that happens in the movie is, she goes into an office and she says: "I am here to see my gynecologist." **Meaning, she is getting a vagina.**

So the movie ends with Barbie reclaiming her sexuality and Ken *not* reclaiming his. Ken doesn't know his masculinity. At the end of the movie, Barbie reclaims her ability to be sexual, but not with any particular Ken.

That's how the movie ends.

The journey in between is fascinating. It is one of the most fascinating journeys you can imagine, but it doesn't get *home*. **It doesn't get to a place where Ken and Barbie have any real reason to come back together.**

In other words, we don't get to level three.

We get to exactly where culture is today: Barbie gets to level two, and claims her independence from Ken. Ken *realizes* that he has to have an identity as Ken, and not be dependent on Barbie, but he never gets there.

KEN IS DESPERATE FOR PATRIARCHY

Ken realizes he should not be dependent on Barbie, so he says, "I want to do patriarchy." Ken goes to the real world, and they tell him about patriarchy. He says, "This is really cool, I like patriarchy. But I'm not a doctor, I'm not a lawyer, I'm not a professional, I'm not a Nobel Prize winner, so patriarchy doesn't work for me so well" (remember, it's talking about the men who are in the manufacturing class). "But I'm going to do patriarchy even without a job."

Does everyone get this?

Ken decides in the movie, "I am going to do patriarchy, but without having a powerful job, just because I am a man." Wow! Does everyone get how pathetic that is and how tragic that is? In other words, Ken is *desperate* to do patriarchy, he says, "I am in charge. Kens are in charge. But I don't have a job, I haven't run a successful business, I'm not a lawyer, I'm not a doctor, I'm not a successful accountant. I'm just doing patriarchy because I am Ken."

My friends, I want you to get the pathos of that and the tragedy of that. None of the reviewers have actually caught the tragedy of this. **This is where the majority of men are in the world today.**

The classical level-one macho man worked at the factory and had a good job. He wasn't an Infotech guy. He was a day laborer or who worked at the factory or in textiles or in cars. There was a huge set of industries around the world, which were industrial revolution, pre-information revolution jobs, that level-one men held, that's what they did.

Then those jobs disappeared. So level-one men didn't know what to do.

There's this huge swath of level-two jobs that are non-manufacturing and non-infotech that are available in the world today, like pharmaceutical, accounting, nursing, teaching, bookkeeping, that women take. All these jobs men aren't taking.

So that's actually how we meet Ken. What does Ken do? He "beaches." Ken hasn't found a way. You just find Ken at a place where he has no job. He's just being *macho*. That's the absurdity of Ken.

Ken is a level-one macho man without a job, so he's not even a role mate. That's why it's such a grotesque critique of the masculine. It's almost male hating.

We're caricaturing Ken. As this grotesque man who's *beaching*. He "beaches off," meaning he masturbates. It's the play in that word. He desperately wants to be a hero, but he's an idiot. He runs into a brick wall. He doesn't have a job. He's not responsible for taking care of any family. **We see just the worst of the masculine.**

Men want patriarchy to be going on—but haven't accomplished any of the achievements of patriarchy. Men want it to be patriarchy just because *I am a man, and I'm just going to embrace my Ken-ness.*

The problem with that is, it doesn't work, because:

- I actually don't have a *Unique Self,*
- I am not *Homo amor,*
- and I don't have a new vision of relationship.

There is no new vision of desire here.

There is no new narrative of desire.

There's no new vision of relationship, what we call the evolution from *role mate to soul mate to whole mate*.[23] We will get to what we mean by "whole mate" later in this chapter.

But this new vision of relationship doesn't exist, it literally doesn't exist. There is no new narrative of desire. There is no sense of what I should be if I can't be a lawyer, a doctor, or a powerful person. What should I do? We have no idea.

Barbie sees no reason to have a man. Barbie doesn't need him. At one point she does say, "Oh, Ken, I'm so sorry that we had girls' night all the time. You can have boys' night sometimes." But when he moves to kiss her, she basically says: *Yo, go away, I'm not interested in that.* But she goes to the real world, and she goes to the gynecologist to get a vagina—meaning *I don't need men for sex, I can do sex myself, I'm going to get my vagina. But why would I need a man for that? Certainly, I don't need not a permanent man for that.*

Ken has this incredible line. He says to Barbie at the most poignant moment, "I always thought this would be our house together." **Ken still somewhat holds the possibility of the love story, but Ken is stuck in level-one relationship and never really gets to level two, let alone level three.**

LEVEL-THREE RELATIONSHIP: FROM ROLE MATE, TO SOUL MATE, TO WHOLE MATE

Barbie and Ken don't get to a level-three masculinity or level-three femininity. They don't get to level-three relationship, or what we call *whole mate relationship*.

---

23 See *Whole Mate: The Future of Relationships* (Gafni, Hubbard, Stein, 2025) and *The Evolution of Love From Quarks to Culture: The Rise of Evolutionary Relationships in Response to the Meta-Crisis* (Gafni, Hubbard, Stein, 2025)

Let's deepen our understanding of what we mean by these levels of relationship.

The evolution of relationship is an expression of the evolution of intimacy. Intimacy evolves *from role mate to soul mate to whole mate.* The drive to not only join genes but to join hearts and ultimately to join genius is the trajectory of the evolution of intimacy in human relationship. "Role mate" is about joining genes, "soul mate" is about joining hearts, and "whole mate" is about joining genius.

Level One: Role Mate Relationship

A "role mate" means simply that each party in the relationship is responsible for a specific set of roles. Historically, men virtually always played the role of protector and provider while women played the role of nurturer and homemaker. The goal of the role-mate relationship was survival and continuity. Survival is an expression of self-love. Role mates come together to ensure that survival. Role mates create a whole that is more than the sum of their parts: they create a family.

Level Two: Soul Mate Relationship

A new level of relationship is born when there is a **soul-mate connection.** Working together for survival and continuity is an insufficient basis for this relationship. In the mid-1960s, **the evolution of intimacy went from role mate to soul mate.** Love evolved, and love began to mean communication and intimacy.

Soul mates were focused not on shared survival but on looking deeply into each other's eyes. Emotional intimacy, radical sharing of wounds, healing, and mutual personal fulfillment are the hallmarks of soul-mate relationships.

- The goal of role-mate relationship is to survive, which is a form of self-love, which extends to partner and family.

- The goal of soul-mate relationship is to transcend loneliness through radical joining with the emotional heart of another.

The evolution from role mate to soul mate is the move from joining genes to joining hearts. Soul mates create a deeper whole than role mates do because the soul-mate relationship includes a new depth of communication and intimacy.

Clearly, evolution never wants to leave the soul-mate relationship behind. But soul mates, in all of their splendor, are not the summit of relationship evolution. There is yet another level—what we believe to be the next level of relationship in the story of the evolution of intimacy.

Level Three: Whole Mate Relationship

This new level of relationship is **the evolutionary movement from soul mate to whole mate.**[24] Whole mate relationships include and transcend the best of role-mate and soul mate relationships. We call it "whole mate" because it is the deepest possible relational whole that one can aspire to at this moment in history.

At some point—for many couples at the leading edge of innovation and transformation—personal fulfillment as the attractor in relationships was no longer satisfying. Soul-mate relationship in its classic form remained a necessary prerequisite for relationship, but it was found to be no longer sufficient. **Couples wanted not only to join genes and hearts but also to join genius.**

They wanted not only to look deeply into each other's eyes but also **to look together at a shared horizon.** *Shared purpose* became central in these relationships. Relationships felt non-erotic without shared vision and values that could be better fulfilled together than apart. This is a new form of love, a new whole, to which previous relationship levels have been leading.

---

24 Ibid., 14. See also: Gafni & Kincaid, *A Return to Eros* (2017), 212–223.

In whole mate relationships, couples seek to join genius to serve the larger whole.

The more that love is evolved in the couple, the wider the whole that they seek to serve. In its highest expression, a whole mate relationship becomes an evolutionary relationship, a relationship in which both parties are living in an evolutionary context.

They experience their relationship as serving the healing and transformation of All-That-Is.

They are evolutionary partners.

Whole mate relationship includes and transcends soul mates.

Barbie and Ken don't need each other for role mate. There are no children, there is no sexuality, they are each on their independent trajectories. Ken seeks a level-two soul mate relationship, but Barbie is not interested, because Barbie says *there is no love story.*

Barbie and Ken don't get to a level-three whole mate relationship, because:

- One, **there is no love story,** Eros is not real, love is not real. They don't feel a sense of the love of Cosmos as *alive and awake in me, in which I participate personally in a larger love story*—none of that is there.
- Two, **they don't have a shared vision.** Role mate itself is also a shared vision. Role mate is a shared vision about my family, *we're raising children together, we're creating a family.* So there is no shared vision for Barbie and Ken.
- Three, they have no relationship to the larger world, **there is no relationship to the larger whole,** so there is no whole mate.

THERE IS NOT ONE DROP OF FEMININE EMPOWERMENT IN *BARBIE*

There is a key moment earlier in the movie, where the men basically make themselves the men in charge, and all the Barbies—the Nobel Prize women, and the doctors, and the lawyers say: "Forget the Nobel Prize, we just want to serve the man. Because we were so lonely having our Nobel Prize, and being lawyers and doctors. We'll just serve the men."

All these accomplished women just go and serve the men, and then there's this key figure Sasha in the movie who wakes the women up from that terrible idea, with this incredible feminist speech.

Do you get what happens?

The women at level two *get lonely.* The women get lonely, and they can't figure out how to get back into a relationship with the man—*so they go back to level one.* But then they realize it doesn't work, and they wake up.

But *what* do they wake up to?

Back into level two, without any level three, **without any new vision of feminine desire.**

In other words, **in the entire *Barbie* movie there is not *one drop* of feminine empowerment.** This is supposed to be the great feminine empowerment movie, but there is *zero* empowerment. It's only empowerment of women to have sex like a man, meaning: *I just have my vagina, but I don't need men. I can have sex however and whenever I want.*

- There is no need for there to be The Universe: A Love Story.
- There is no need for there to be relationship.
- I'm going to go back to being a doctor, lawyer, Nobel Prize winner.
- I'm going to go back to the real world, I'm going to embrace my humanity and my death, but *why would I be in a relationship?*

That's actually exactly where the movie gets to. It does not get beyond that—because that's as far as culture has gotten.

This movie is supposed to be the great movie of feminine empowerment, but there is not one second of feminine empowerment in this movie—because *feminine empowerment* **means you are empowered** *as a woman.* To be empowered as a woman means: *Yes, I can be a doctor, for sure I can be a lawyer, because men and women can both be doctors and lawyers, but I also want to be a lawyer in a way that's not the way a man is a lawyer. I want to be just as good a lawyer, but I want to bring in my feminine. What is my feminine? What does it actually mean to be a woman?*

Why is it that there are anatomical differences between men and women, why are there hormonal differences between men and women, and why are there obviously physical differences between men and women? The world *did* produce masculine and feminine—so *I don't want to be a lawyer, doctor, Nobel Prize winner, and* give up *my feminine. I want to* integrate *my feminine.*

There is no feminine empowerment in Barbie. There is no masculine empowerment in Barbie.

What does it mean to be a man when the men are trying to do patriarchy without a job? It's pathetic. Do you get how pathetic that image is? Basically, it mocks men. There is not one good male hero in the movie. It's filled with women heroes, which is why people say this is feminine empowerment. **The heroes are all women, that's true, but there is no vision of feminine empowerment.** You have women heroes, but they're not being feminine. They've just become men. **There is no integration, no new narrative of what it means to be the new woman.**

Who is the level-three woman in the movie? There's no level-three woman, and there is no level-three man. There isn't even a level-two soul-mate relationship between men and women. **The women still are the heroes, and the men are actually tragic and pathetic**. There isn't one positive image of the man in the movie.

For example, when Barbie goes to the real world, and she goes to the Mattel big office building, and they get to the office where all the board members are men. And the movie mocks all of the men—it's a terrible vision of men. These are the patriarchy guys, and they are shallow, and they are superficial, and they are idiots.

There is this key woman in the movie, a woman and her daughter—*they* are the heroes, but when we meet her husband at the end of the movie, he is also depicted as an idiot.

Then there is one big action scene of men, where the men are fighting with each other—the women actually get the men to fight with each other. Since the men can't get women, they fight with each other, and there's this huge, hilarious battle scene between the men fighting with tennis rackets—an insane, choreographed, very funny, but very tragic and pathetic scene.

I want us to get where the movie goes:

- **The woman is the hero.** She has succeeded in being a man, but she hasn't embraced any new dimension of the feminine. Even in sexuality, she is like a man. **There is no new experience of feminine desire, of feminine power.**
- **There is no vision of the masculine at all.** There are no masculine heroes in the entire movie, which is exactly where we are in culture.
- **The feminine is identified with the good.** The feminine has no shadow. She doesn't need a man.
- **The masculine is pathetic.** He's trying to do patriarchy without a job, essentially. This is an incredibly pathetic view of a man.

LEVEL-THREE RELATIONSHIPS: SYNERGIZING LINES AND CIRCLES

Another way of speaking about these levels of femininity/masculinity, is to say that at level one he is *a line* and she is *a circle.* He's thrusting forward and taking care of everything and running the show, and she's supporting, she's nurturing,

Then in level-two, line and circle, masculine and feminine, men and women, are kind of in *balance.* They're both raising the kids, they're both working, and they have deep communication.

This first level of relationship is what we call *role mate relationship,* the second level is what we call *soul mate relationship.* But then the third level of relationship, which we call *whole mate relationship,* is when he reverts to the strong masculine. He has incorporated the side of him that reads Rumi, he has incorporated the soul dimension in his being, it's an enlightened sense of wholeness. He is thrusting forward powerfully, but from an enlightened place. Not from a dominating, level-one, separate-self place, but from an Evolutionary Unique Self place.

In this level-three whole mate relationship, she is *radiance* and *beauty,* but the difference is that **in level-one *role mate,* she has to seduce him in order to be secure.** But then at level-three she has integrated her line quality. **Instead of trying to seduce him, she is *Fuck* radiant.**

She is *Fuck.*[25]

She is the radiance of Cosmos.

She has moved from a separate self, *Let me seduce you, to get you, and I'll take care of the kids,* to *I am the radiant She and I enchant Reality.* Her circle radiance is not in contradiction to her conquering line. **She has integrated the line and circle.**

---

25 See *The Abridged Phenomenology of Eros, Volume One* (forthcoming*), Essay One, On the Word Fuck.* See an early version of that essay by on Substack: "Bypassing the Energy of F--k Creates Abuse," https://marcgafni.substack.com/p/bypassing-fuck-creates-abuse.

- **Level one:** He is line, she is circle.
- **Level two:** They try to do line and circle together. They're each adopting some of each other's qualities, but it gets very neutral. He's not really a line anymore, he's trying to be a circle. She's not really a circle anymore, she is trying to be a line. He is taming his line down. She's not really filled with the *Fuck* of her *radiance*. They're in this mutuality, this sweet partnership, but there's no *Fucking*.
- **Level three:** they each reclaim their core, masculine and feminine, and they have integrated the other side.

That is what we are calling level three *whole mate relationship*.

At level three, you integrate your lines and circles, in a way where you're not just *balancing* your lines and circles, you're **synergizing your lines and circles.** At level three, men and women become this powerful force where she is full-on circle and he is full-on line, even as they've integrated, each other's line and circle qualities.

So whole mate is the *hieros gamos* of line and circle. It's a full *hieros gamos*. In other words, soul mate is more like a *balance* of line and circle. It's not a full *hieros gamos*. Whole mate is the synergy, the full *hieros gamos*, of line and circle. That's the subtle point here.

LINES AND CIRCLES IN KEN AND BARBIE

On her way to level-two, Barbie has moved out of her passive *circle*. She has moved out of just being the nurturing circle. She has moved out of *seducing the man in order to get security*, and just raising the kids.

She steps into her own power. She claims her own line. The Barbie stories are exactly that. She's a president and she's a doctor and she's a researcher and she's an astronaut.

The Barbie dolls are precisely this move from level-one to level-two femininity. Meaning, from a kind of a classical circle role mate, toward a level-two role, where they've claimed their line. So they're now thrusting forward in the world. They're now successful in the world. They're now accomplishing in the world. So they're in the classical mode of third-wave feminism, where women have claimed their professional place in the world. **They have claimed their line energy.**

But they haven't succeeded in going back and claiming their feminine, their *Fuck*, their beauty, their radiance—they don't even have genitals.

Barbie claims her line, but her relationship to her feminine gets confused. On the one hand, she remains beautiful. She wears great clothes, and she dresses well, and she has great shoes. And she always shows up perfectly.

Yet Barbie doesn't go to the soul-mate place of vulnerability and woundedness and openness. She doesn't want to create relationship with Ken. She's not looking for Ken to read *Rumi* with her.

She's not moved by him. She's not allured to him. **That's the tragedy of Barbie and Ken.**

Barbie might actually be interested in a true level-two Ken, but he doesn't show up. He goes back to patriarchy. He might actually be able to find Barbie in a level two, if she helped him open the door, but he feels (and is) utterly rejected by her, like when he's reaching to kiss her and she said, *It's girls' night, every night, forever.* Meaning, *I'm completely not interested in who you are. I don't see you. I'm not interested in your masculinity.*

Level three would mean, that Barbie is *actually* beautiful. She's not just dolled-up beautiful. She's actually alluring. She's madly in love. At level three, Barbie is going to *make love* with Ken—she's going to *invite* Ken.

Instead, what Barbie says to Ken is, "It's girls' night, every night, forever."

Level-three femininity means, you don't seduce the masculine (level one), but you enchant the masculine—you are radiance itself. You are the unique Field of Eros.

She is stuck at a distortion of level two, which is, *Fuck you Ken, I'm a line, and there's no place for you here. I'm not in the old role-mate relationship. I've claimed my place, I've claimed my line.*

She did not get close to level three, where she reclaims her feminine radiance in relationship to the masculine and to the whole world. She did not get there. None of the Barbie women have.

What about Ken? Ken doesn't even get to level-two. But it is actually a little more complex.

Ken is *interested* in getting to level two. He's trying to find his way. Ken is level one. He's the strong, macho guy, but *he actually really loves Barbie.* He wants to find Barbie. He's looking for Barbie. He's looking for her from a level-one place. He doesn't look at her in a way where he deeply *sees* her, where he wants to truly communicate with her, where he wants to have depth with her, or where he wants to share their wounds, as we would expect in a level-two *soul mate* relationship. We don't see that, but what we do feel is a *yearning* for that. **We feel Ken wants to get to level two, and he doesn't know how to get there.**

We see very clearly Barbie claiming her line energy, but we don't completely see Ken claiming his *circle* energy.

We do see fragrances of it, the way that he's dressing and how his hair is cool—he's being a little feminine. But we don't see a sensitive New Age guy. He's not a sensitive New Age guy. He's not like, *Let's do communication. Let's talk things through.* He doesn't do any of that.

Now the question is, does he not get there because Barbie rejected him and he's hurt? Ken has moments of vulnerable opening, like in the "I'm Just Ken" song, but he gets slammed shut. He gets mocked. So Ken gets angry. Ken is bitter. **Ken is angry because he can't find his way to Barbie.**

Ken doesn't quite know what he's doing wrong, but Barbie also doesn't quite know how to guide him in.

Barbie herself, when she claims her line, loses a lot of her circle. That's the paradox of *Barbie*. She's dressed perfectly. Ken is allured to her. She still has some of her feminine, but **she doesn't know how to embrace the masculine.** She doesn't know how to be *truly alluring*, how to be truly *generous*, how to be truly *enchanting*. That's level three. She doesn't know how to get there.

A TASTE OF LEVEL-THREE MASCULINE & FEMININE

At level-three *whole mate relationship*, the feminine reclaims its full feminine.

It's a **full inhabiting of feminine radiance.** It's not a separate-self role, but rather:

> *I am love itself.*
>
> *I am the Field of Outrageous Love, unique and incarnate in me.*
>
> *I enchant Reality.*
>
> *I dazzle Reality with my beauty.*
>
> *I invite Reality into the depth of my feminine holding.*
>
> *I hold all of Reality between my breasts.*
>
> *I suckle Reality even as my phallus is throbbing, and I thrust forward to create in the world.*

I'm both thrusting forward and I'm embracing and holding and radiant.

The quality of my True Self, Unique Self, and Evolutionary Unique Self are all at play through my feminine.

So my feminine is radiant, Outrageous Love, generosity, enchanting. I enchant with my full being.

*If I seduce, it's not a low-level seduction (let me seduce you in order to get ahead in the world), it is **the seduction of the Goddess**. I'm seducing you into this in unimaginable beauty.*

I'm seducing you to your highest self.

Those are the qualities of level-three femininity that *Barbie* doesn't get to.

Level-three masculinity for Ken would be:

- He has a sense of purpose on his own, not just to Barbie.
- He is in service to the whole.
- He is both **fully in his male power** and yet madly devoted to her.
- He sees her in her strength.
- He's delighted when she emerges in her own power.
- He's insanely happy when he sees her beauty, his whole heart melts.
- The nature of their erotic relationship, is such that he can be strong and dominating, and he can also be completely tender and soft. He can be radically attuned, and feel everything that she might possibly want him to feel. He can be the radically strong, thrusting open masculine at the same time. He can move between them.
- He's madly delighted by her power, he's interested in her power. He doesn't want to dominate her. He wants her power to emerge. He wants her to be powerful.

That is level-three masculine. He has his line, he has a circle, he is not *balanced* between his line and circle, they're actually completely *synergized into one*. That's the ultimate level three, which is very rare. But the movie doesn't even hint towards it.

Here's another way to put it:

Role mate is when the man is in the classical line. He's moving forward, he's directional. He's making distinctions. He's fulfilling his role. He is the deciding force. He's somewhat aggressive, but he's also making the decisions. He's the protector, he's the aggressor, he's in charge. He's very deeply in touch with his line qualities, but not really in touch with his feminine qualities at all.

Then, at level-two soul mate, he still has line quality, but it's a little more attenuated, a little less thrusting. It's *balanced* with this circle quality, which is a softer quality, where he wants to communicate and listen, and he's willing to process. You would never hear a level-one guy say, *do you need to process now?* **At level one, he has sex, rolls over and goes to sleep. He's barely aware if she has an orgasm or not.** At level two, he's like, *How does that feel for you, honey?* But he has to do it in a way that's real.

So he's actually in touch with his feelings, he's in touch with his vulnerability. He's in touch with her emotions. He wants to hear her vulnerability and her emotions. The classical level-two movie is a movie called *Love Story.* They're both willing to be committed, willing to be vulnerable, willing to share their wounding, they look deeply in each other's eyes. That's level two. He's both line and circle together, but they're not yet integrated. His line's a little attenuated, he's beginning to develop circle. They haven't been integrated. But he has circle qualities coming online.

His line gets a little softer, his line gets a little less aggressive, a little less powerful. He certainly wouldn't want to ravish her. He's very careful. He probably makes sure he gets consent at every stage. He's very careful not to offend her. He couldn't be sharp. He certainly wouldn't slap her in sex play. That'd be like wildly offensive to him. He's all about her. He is the sensitive New Age guy. That's who he is.

But she is not that *wet,* she is not that aroused—there's no polarity between them.

She doesn't feel his *Fuck*.
She doesn't feel his force.
She doesn't feel his passion.
She doesn't feel his demand of the world.

She wants to feel him radically committed, willing to go to the edge, willing to fight for something that matters.

She needs to feel his edge. She needs to feel his throbbing. She is yearning for his demand, his radical steadiness, his fundamental directionality, his thrusting forward.

He's afraid of those qualities at this point. He's still has some of them, but he has left a lot of them in level-one role mate spaces. He says, *I can't, I'm this kind of soft, sensitive, New Age guy.*

When he gets to level three, he reclaims those level-one qualities again. Now he's thrusting and he's powerful and he's dominating in the good sense of the word, and he might even spank her in sex play, but his heart is completely open—not like some kind of level-one brutality. They spark each other with incredibly open, tender hearts, even if it is fierce.

It's a completely new synergy.

At level three, they each reclaim their line and circle qualities. She **reclaims her circle.** She reclaims the circle from level one, but on a much **higher level of consciousness, much more powerful.** Now, she's radiant, she's enchanting. She's not, *look at me*, needing attention or safety. She's like, *I'm the Goddess.*

For example, Trinity, in *The Matrix*, she's not the devoted wife. **She's level three. She has her man's back. She'll do anything for her man. She's this powerful, *fucking* fierce, level-three character.**

She is beauty itself.

She is the *Fuck* of Cosmos moving through her. She is going to hold her man like her man holds her. It's very beautiful. It's not *I'm devoted to my man*, it's more that *I'm holding my man*.

CHAPTER 4

THE MOCKING OF
THE HERO

THE OLD RELATIONSHIP STYLE HAS BEEN
DEMONIZED AS PATRIARCHY

Let's go back and look at level one—where did it come from?

As we discussed in chapter 3, the *Barbie* movie opens with the old-style Barbie dolls, which stand for the old relationship style (when I say "the old relationship style," we are not looking at the last 5,000 years or 10,000 years, just at the last few 100 years as a snippet of culture).

In the old relationship style world, you had the old Barbie dolls, who were, in some sense or another, what we would call level-one relationships, or *role mate relationships*:

- Men were out there making a living. They were protectors and providers.
- Women were childbearers: they were holding the baby, they were nurturing, and they were creating the household.

We had an old relationship style, that broke down in many ways. There were moments in history when women were significantly involved in commerce and other areas. This is not a *full* historical read—but in general, you could easily and accurately say that **over the past thousand years, there was a core relationship deal**. Amazonian Queens and Wonder Woman movies aside—those are exceptions (that's why the movies go wild), but the basic model has been some version of this relationship deal.

There was a *polarity,* **a movement between men and women in the world, in which they each *needed* each other in a particular way.** This relationship structure may have started in the world of farming, or maybe the world of early agriculture, maybe early agrarian, which is farming with plows, maybe even horticultural, maybe even earlier in history—it's not entirely clear. I'm not going to do the anthropology now, though it's quite an interesting conversation. But there is some version of this relationship deal in place forever.

This relationship deal is now demonized as *patriarchy*. But that's not quite accurate.

The level-one deal was not a bunch of weak women dominated by a bunch of bad men who forced women into this agreement, as Janet Chavez and other feminist scholars point out. No, this relationship deal came into being for many reasons, including:

- The need for safe childbirth—and the difficulty of having safe childbirth once we moved from early horticultural handheld tools to heavy plough tools. Miscarriage became far more possible, and the natural upper body strength of men being naturally stronger made more difference
- The difference in biological, physical structure between men and women: Women have breasts that lactate and feed babies and wombs that actually grow babies.

This difference—combined with socio-cultural issues, economic issues, and also with interior senses—created this relationship deal. **There was**

much that was beautiful in this relationship deal and there was much that was terrible, that was a horror, which is fairly critiqued by people who label this deal as patriarchy.

This critique is absolutely true.

Obviously, in this relationship deal, the feminine, after a certain amount of time, was disenfranchised. Until 120 years ago, women didn't vote in the world. The most sophisticated Western men in the world, even 120 years ago, who supported women emerging, still said women can't vote. *That it would be absurd to have women vote!* That's just to give you a sense of this, just one fragrance; this is the tip of an iceberg.

There was a lot to critique about this relationship deal—but it is *also* true that it emerged because of a set of economic, social, interior, exterior factors that came together. **This became, for a period of time, the way to create a stable unit called *a family*, and that family held together society and allowed society to evolve.**

That's about where we are.

The initial scene of *Barbie,* where we see young girls playing housewife, is alluding to all of this. The first few seconds in *Barbie* are alluding to this whole world.

KEN IN THE WORLD OF IDEALIZED FEMINISM

Then *Barbie* says that there is a new world that has emerged, which is the emergence of second-wave feminism (although the movie doesn't call it that), in which women are empowered.

Now, who reading this is a feminist?

I hope all of us.

Second-wave feminism is this notion that:

- Women need to claim their place, that their place has been split off from them.
- Women should be winning Nobel Prizes.
- Women should be, if they want to be, doctors.
- If they want to be, they should be researchers.
- If they want to be, they should be presidents.
- If they want to be, they should be senators.
- If they want to be, they should be pharmacologists.

It was a true emergence, and there is this common sense that we all agree on this. There is the sense that all problems have been solved. **That's what the beginning of *Barbie* is: everything has been solved, it's all good.**

In the beginning of *Barbie* we see a whole set of scenes, where women are doctors and entrepreneurs. There is a scene where we see women in the White House and one of the Barbie dolls gives a speech about how there is no contradiction between logic and feelings, how they are both perfectly integrated, and play beautifully in the world. There is this idealized sense of a successful feminism, represented by the entire new line of Barbie dolls, all in emancipated positions in societies.

It's all good, we've arrived at this great liberation and this great new world.

That's how *Barbie* begins.

Then it starts to get interesting. We get to this strange moment: *there is something wrong.*

Remember, when we first meet Ken, the narrator says: *Barbie has a great day every day. Ken only has a great day when Barbie looks at him.* Ken only feels good if he is in Barbie's gaze, if Barbie looks at him.

We see Ken at the beach. It's this very subtle and beautiful moment. And then Ken says: *Hey, Barbie, check me out!*

He takes his surfboard, and he runs headlong into the water while Barbie is watching him. Of course, he's not exactly looking out, and he smashes into a concrete barrier and is taken to the hospital, and Barbie goes with him to the hospital and says: *Ken, you're so brave!*

What is she saying? What's happening here?

BARBIE LIBERATED HERSELF FROM THE MALE GAZE OF KEN

Barbie is in Barbie land. Barbie goes down to her car—she goes out of her house, falls perfectly into her car. Her makeup is perfect. She looks beautiful. But if you notice, something has shifted:

She is not that concerned with Ken looking at her. **Although she is being perfect, she's not being perfect for Ken.** There's this advancement—she is being perfect *for herself*—and in some sense, that's a very deep and beautiful advance.

- Barbie is not getting dressed to be alluring to Ken.
- She is not being sexy to be alluring to Ken.
- She is not picking beautiful colors of clothes to be alluring to Ken.

As we know, she's actually not interested in Ken.

On one level, that's an advance. That's an evolutionary step forward: I am being beautiful because I want to be beautiful, because I want to feel my beauty, and I want to feel my delight. It's a beautiful step forward. It feels great.

There is also a tragedy here.

Because here is the story. Do you *really* get dressed up the same way when you are by yourself? Occasionally we do—but do we *regularly* get dressed up the same way when we're by ourselves?

The answer is, most of us don't. Sometimes we do, because we want to feel good. I try to put on good clothes every day that feel good, that are relaxed—but if I'm utterly by myself in the house, I'll still get dressed, but

I'll pay a little bit less attention. Is it wrong that I'll pay a little bit less atten-tion? Is it that I am disconnected with my own individuality? Well, maybe, in part.

- It *is* important to get dressed up, and it is important to have a sense of *self-love,* and it's important to *individuate.* That's all true.
- And it's also not wrong that we live in a relationship. It's not wrong.

I just want to track this:

- There's a level one of role-mate relationship, where the woman is getting dressed up for the man and being beautiful for the man, but where she's not connected to her own power, she's not connected to her own Eros, she's not connected to her own sensuality. It is all for the man, which is, in some sense, degraded and pathological. It's an expression of an insidious, tyrannical cosmetics industry. That is an oppression of the feminine and it's degrading to the feminine, and the feminine does need to move beyond that. Yes, big yes on that, big yes.
- And there is a **level-two relationship** where individuation hap-pens, where she moves beyond that, and the woman says: *Hey, I'm not going to do any of those things only for the man.* It might have to do with how she dresses, it might have to do with her clothes, and it might have to do with makeup or no makeup. Sometimes feminism is anti-lipstick and anti *any* sort of cosmetic. There's this rejection of the degraded notion of the feminine. That's level two.
- But then, level two can *pathologize*—this is already in the beginning of the movie. I am getting dressed up irrespective of my relationship to other, whether it is to the man or to my beloved.

Again, the *Barbie* movie ignores the LGBTQ+ world. That's the one sense in which the *Barbie* movie is completely politically incorrect. It's all about Ken and Barbie, and it freeze-frames on classical—what we would call *normative*—heterosexuality. That's *Barbie*'s frame.

But let's talk about a wider frame. Let's not talk about just Barbie and Ken. Let's just talk about *a wider love story.* It's Barbie and Barbie, it's Ken and Jack, it's Barbie and Melissa. In other words, **there is a love story, and so there is some sense in which I *do* get dressed for my beloved.** There is a sense that there is a *relationship,* and there's a sense of *Reality is relationship.*

To sum up the first point: already in the beginning of *Barbie,* there's this sense in which **Barbie is no longer concerned to be in the gaze of Ken.** She has **liberated herself from the male gaze,** which is super beautiful and important—but there is a *shadow* to it.

Now, by itself, you can't tell if this is a shadow or not—but you have this first insidious sense, I got it as soon as I watched the movie: this is a great step forward, but Barbie is completely unconcerned with her beloved, whoever her beloved is, whether her beloved is Melissa or Barbie-2 or Ken.

She is not concerned, because she has no beloved.

She is just in her own self-referential *girls' night every night, forever!*

Constant delight, no relationship to other, no notion of Reality as relationship—or at least, of **Reality being a yearning love story, where I reach out *beyond my biology*,** meaning, I reach out beyond my biology, and I'm yearning to love someone that's not my biology, that's not my daughter, that's not my brother.

I am yearning to love because love moves in me.

That notion of loving transcends race and transcends biology.

Because then, I *do* get all dressed up for you sometimes. That's part of what that relationship is—not in its pathological sense, but its beautiful sense.

But in *Barbie* that's all wiped out.

It's very subtle.

BARBIE DISMISSES THE ONTOLOGY OF RELATIONSHIP

Do you see how it has now been *reversed*? Ken has now become what used to be the *level-one* or *role-mate* woman. Ken now says:

If you're not looking at me, Barbie, I don't exist.

Wow! So Ken has now adopted and internalized the pathologized version of relationship level one. *If you're not looking at me, Barbie, I don't exist.*

Wow, that's not quite right!

Ken gets relationship, he gets that relationship is real—but he is a caricatured and pathologized version of relationship.

These are literally the first scenes, if you're reading carefully. **In the first scene, *Barbie* dismisses the ontology of relationship.** It *seems* like an evolutionary move forward, but there's also a deep shadow to it. There is a stepping out of the notion that *Reality is relationships*. And then, Ken is appearing in that old pathologized version of feminine level-one relationships.

Barbie is going to correctly say to Ken later, *you have to be Ken*—and that's true, that's a partially right thing. You *do* need to be Ken, and Ken does not *only* exist in relationship to Barbie.

There is a notion of *autonomy*. There's not only *communion*.

- **Intimate communion** is one dimension of a love story.
- There is a second dimension of a love story, which is: I am individuated, I am self-loving, I am committed to my own perpetuation, the perpetuation of my own Unique Self. That's self-love, that's **autonomy.**

Ken has to be Ken, and Barbie has to be Barbie. That's absolutely true. But that's only one dimension of the love story.

Barbie is going beyond that to say: **love is not real**. There is no real love story between people who are allured to each other. Allurement is not real in Cosmos, attraction is not real, intimate communion is not real.

What *is* there in *Barbie*?

- There is autonomy.
- There is *me being me*.
- There's this contrived sense which—in *Barbie*—we're going to call self-love—but it's really just, *be me*, because everything else is made-up and the only thing that seems to be real is that I am here, so I should love me in some way.

There is no "Barbie + Ken," there is only autonomy.

It's not even framed as a genuine self-love story; there is no coming back together. The overwhelming message of this movie is going to be that "Barbie + Ken" is not real; there's no ontology to "Barbie + Ken." There is no real love story.

We will see, scene by scene, how this is constructed. We're going to go into the laboratory of culture and see how culture speaks.

The way the movie does that in the beginning is that:

1. **It pathologizes the notion of Barbie existing in Ken's gaze** (which is in part correct—that is pathology).
2. It then sets up Ken as the inverse: **Ken now *only* exists in Barbie's gaze.**

It doesn't create a next step, where:

I *do* get dressed up for Ken, and Ken *does* get dressed up for me.

We *do* live in relationship to each other.

We do want to be in relationship to each other.

We do want to be moved by each other's beauty and depth.

We do want to be aroused by each other's voice.

We actually *do* live in relationship, because Reality is allurement, and Reality *is* relationship—all the way down and all the way up the evolutionary chain. But that is subtly denied, already in the very beginning of *Barbie*.

It's going to get much more dramatic.

KEN'S MALE DESIRE TO BE A HERO IS MOCKED

So what is happening when Barbie says "You're so brave!" right after Ken smashes into a concrete barrier. Ken says to Barbie, "Did you see that?" In other words, *did you see what I did for you?* He is trying to impress Barbie, because he only exists in her gaze. Barbie goes with him to the doctor and says: "Oh, Ken, you're so brave." And we wonder, what does Ken do for her to call him brave? But she is not really relating to Ken, she is just being polite. It's a mocking line, it's not real. She is mocking him—not directly, but it's a mockery.

- She is not really *moved* by Ken.
- She is not *aroused* by Ken.
- She is not *allured* to Ken.

She does the "polite society" thing because she is the perfect woman who does the polite society thing, but there's no depth to it. There is no resonance to it. There is no sincerity to it. **Ken is not really a hero to Barbie**. This is really important.

- He is *not* being brave.
- He is *not* being courageous.
- He has done something insanely stupid and idiotic. He ran headlong into a concrete wall, essentially a concrete barrier, without looking.
- He's pretending heroism—for no good reason other than to attract the attention of the feminine, which is considered to be absurd in the movie because there is no love story.

So, basically **male heroism is reduced to the man trying to weirdly get the attention of the woman.** She kind of fawns over him, but she's actually mocking him. She knows he's an idiot.

Ken wants to be a hero, but he doesn't know how to be a hero.

Ken doesn't know how to get wounded for real.

He doesn't know how to get injured for real.

There is a subtle condescension. He doesn't know how to be a hero, but he desperately *wants* to be a hero. In whose eyes? In Barbie's eyes. And Barbie says *you're so brave*, but she doesn't mean it, it's a condescending mockery.

He desperately wants to be a hero. He wants to be seen in her gaze, and he feels like *I don't exist out of your gaze.*

Now, is Ken right that he doesn't exist out of her gaze?

He's absolutely wrong, and... he's absolutely right.

If Reality is relationships, we actually don't exist out of relationship.

That's actually true.

Ken is not wrong, he is just a pathologized version of that truth.

The entire movie is going to caricature the notion that Reality is relationships. It's going to caricature the notion that there *is* a real love story—and place that notion in the eyes of an idiotic Ken.

This notion that Reality is relationship and the notion that I only exist in your gaze, is placed in the mouth of the idiotic Ken.

The notion that *the love story is real* is going to be the demonized claim of patriarchy—we will deepen this in chapter 5. Patriarchy is going to be the voice for the Reality of The Universe: A Love Story. The notion that there *is* a Ken and Barbie love story is going to be patriarchy's voice. Do you see how subtle that is?

That begins already in this scene of Ken at the beach, in which this **male desire to be a hero is mocked,** because there are no heroes.

Hanna Rosin anticipates this in the book I mentioned earlier, *The End of Men and the Rise of Women.* One of the themes in *Barbie* is **the ridiculousness of the male desire to be a hero, the mocking of the male desire to be a hero.**

The other scene in the movie that mocks male heroism is the scene on the beach where the men fight. **It's a complete mocking of men fighting on beaches.** For example, the men storming the beaches of Normandy in World War II—which is the opening scene of the movie *Saving Private Ryan.* The men storming the beach. In *Barbie,* it's portrayed as this weird fight between men on the beach, which is utterly absurd.

Finally, the **rest of the male idiots in the movie** are the entire board of Mattel (the company that created Barbie). There's this wild scene, where they're chasing after Barbie. They get to a turnstile, and you have to scan a card or something if you want to get through. The men can't get through, and they are mocked as idiots.

The point is, male heroism is completely destroyed, because all the men are idiots in the movie.

LOVERS WANT TO BE HEROES

This is so deep, my friends, and this is going to get deeper and deeper. It's going to get crazy deep.

See, I want to be a hero—but **I want to be a hero *for you*.** I want my heroism to be *received.* There's this enormous desire to be a hero.

Now, Barbie doesn't want to get dressed for the masculine (a great step forward), but she also doesn't want to be a hero for the masculine.

- She wants to be creative.
- She wants to have a full life.
- She wants to be successful.
- She wants to be a great entrepreneur, and she wants to be fulfilled.

All of that is beautiful and a great evolutionary step forward—but she loses the truth of *Reality is relationship*. The pathologized version of that truth then appears in Ken.

Ken stands for the desire of the beloved to be a hero. He is the *line* expression. He is the engendered masculine expression, but it lives in all of us. That desire to be a hero is an essential dimension of a love story.

> *There is no love story without our desire to be a hero for each other. The love story means we want to be a hero for each other. Lovers want to be heroes.*

If you are a lover, you want to be a hero. That's the nature of being a lover.

Ken wants Barbie to look at him, and he wants to be a hero—but Barbie doesn't see any hero, and she blithely, superciliously, condescendingly praises him, as he idiotically smashes into this brick barrier.

What does Ken do for a living? Nothing.

What does Ken create? Nothing.

What does Ken do? He *beaches*. It's a verb, he *beaches*.

He doesn't *do* anything. He just shows up. Ken is always looking great, but he is not doing anything. He beaches. He's *not* a hero, and she's like: *Oh, you're so brave.* Wow!

Now just check this out for a second.

At level one, we have this old pathologized role mate, and that role is: the man is the hero; he is the protector-provider. The woman tries to look beautiful for the man, and she is the nurturer. She creates the family, she bears the children—but the man is still called the hero. That is correctly rejected by *Barbie*: **The man *is* the hero, but so is the woman.**

First off, the woman has to be in her own beauty for its own sake. She gets dressed up for herself. Yes, that's beautiful.

But then *Barbie* pathologizes the very notion of the relationship between Barbie and Ken, and we are going to see that pathologizing of that relationship deepen in ten ways. We're just getting started.

Ken becomes the pathologized version of level-one role mate relationship. *I only exist in the gaze of the beloved*, becomes Ken, not Barbie.

And then, there is no hero:

- Barbie is not really a hero, she's just *being successful.*
- Ken is not a hero. He doesn't *do* anything, he just beaches. Wow!

That's where we are.

SOUL MATES OUTSIDE THE FIELD OF VALUE

Now, we're going to do a little more foreshadowing.

Barbie is critiquing level-one relationship. It begins to examine level-two relationship, but portrays it to be pathological.

There is no sense that we go from *role mate* to *soul mate,* meaning this beautiful love story between beloveds: whether it is men and women, women and women, men and men. That's actually what culture *did*, it did go from role mate to soul mate. But what Barbie is saying is: Soul mate is bullshit. There is no love story.

Now, stay really close:

Implicit in the cultural story of soul mate was that soul mate lives outside of the Field of Value.

In the entire movie there is nothing of what CosmoErotic Humanism names as the "Field of Value." **There is no sense of what is intrinsically good and what really matters. And so there can be no real love story.**

Value creates responsibility. When I have value, I *inconvenience* myself, and I recognize that this value of love is huge and beautiful, and it *demands* something from me.

- Intimacy creates *obligation.*
- Intimacy creates *radical commitment.*
- Intimacy creates the willingness to *sacrifice,* to bracket yourself for the sake of your own transformation. *I bracket myself in order to give to you*—that's what love means.

This way love, or intimacy, does not stand on its own but participates in a larger Field of Value (obligation, commitment, and sacrifice).

There is no love outside of the Field of Value.

Postmodernity tries to claim the love story without the Field of Value—but postmodernity is rooted in modernity, which actually made the same move but hid it.

Modernity *assumes* love is a value. Postmodernity says, no, we are going to say *I love you*, but actually, love is not real.

We killed all the Gods and Goddesses.

We killed value.

But we thought we could kill value and retain only *one* value.

Which one? Love.

We'll kill all the Goddesses except for Aphrodite, except for the Goddess of Love.

As we said before, in culture, we moved from role mate (in different versions over the last 100,000 years) into soul mate (which is only in the last several decades, mid-60s into the 70s and 80s):

- John Grey writes: *Men are from Mars, Women are from Venus,* about soul-mate relationships.
- Harville Hendrix writes his book, *Getting the Love You Want,* about soul-mate relationships. It's about communication and vulnerability.
- Gary Chapman writes a book called *The Five Love Languages,* which is about soul-mate relationship. It's all about language and communication, which is a whole new quality of relationship.

That's soul mate. In culture, there is the attempt to enact this new field of relation, which is about this great love story, but they try to enact this love story *outside of the Field of Value.*

At the same time that we move from role mate to soul mate, we also move from modernity to postmodernity, and postmodernity says, there is no Field of Value.

Postmodernity says, there is no Field of Value, nothing is really real, it's all made up.

Ah, but *something* has to be real.

What are we going to make real? Oh, the *romantic* love story. Postmodernity says: *all that's left is the "love story."*

- But the actual story that dominates culture, that really drives us in all of our creative lives and all of our status lives and all of our social lives, is **the success story**: rivalrous conflict governed by win/lose metrics.

- We feel its emptiness, so we have a booby prize, the "love story"—but at the same time we don't really believe love is real. This is what we mean when we say, we killed all the Goddesses except for Aphrodite. **Postmodernity deconstructed the Field of Value, trying to keep the value of (romantic) love alive as a booby prize—but you can't keep Aphrodite alive when you decontextualized her from the Field of Value.**

This is deep, friends, this is so crazy deep. We can't decontextualize love from the Field of Value and say *I love you*—**there is no *I love you* without value**.

Barbie is an expression of the fact that Aphrodite—love as a real value—has to die if the Field of Value is deconstructed.

KEN + BARBIE IS THE NATURE OF REALITY

The point of the *Barbie* movie is:

There is ultimately no love story; there is no Ken + Barbie. You thought you could kill all the gods except for Aphrodite, and the great love story of Aphrodite will remain. It will not.

It will not unless it's rooted in the Field of Value.

The Field of Value is a Field of Eros.

Eros is a value of Cosmos.

Eros, love, and intimacy are First Principles and First Values of Cosmos.

Eros, love, and value are the structure of Reality—

- all the way from subatomic particles,
- all the way through the world of matter,
- all the way through the world of the biosphere, biology,
- all the way through the depth of the self-reflective human mind.

In other words, Ken + Barbie is true *not* because it's a human contrivance.

Ken + Barbie is true because Ken + Barbie is the nature of Reality, all the way up and all the way down the evolutionary chain.

Reality is ErosValue all the way up and all the way down.

You cannot cut off the flower at its root and expect the flower to bloom. The rose wilts after a few years.

You can't cut off love from its roots in the Field of ErosValue and expect love to remain real.

Along comes *Barbie* and says, *you know what, my friends,* **there is no love story**—and it chills the very *heart* of culture. And because there is no love story, there are no heroes.

It correctly critiques—that's the paradox—this ascription of the hero to only the masculine, but it does it by *caricaturing* the masculine desire to be a hero. The idiot man wants to be a hero. For doing what? For beaching.

There is no notion that heroism could be real, that the hero is real, and that there is a new vision in which both men and women are heroes—both lines and circles.

And again, when I say *lines and circles*, I refer to the notion of line as a geometric quality of Reality, the quality that later got *engendered* as the masculine:

- The line **divides**,

- and the line creates appropriate **hierarchies of responsibility,**
- and the line creates **language,**
- and the line creates **the movement forward.**

The line is the storyline. The line is a very powerful instrument of Reality.

Then there is the circle:

- the circle goes for **depth,**
- the circle *contains,*
- the circle *includes,*
- the circle also has the circular. It goes round and round until it can go even deeper, and it gets the cycle of life.
- and the circle *holds.*

Lines and circles are these two qualities which are way *before* masculine and feminine. Lines and circles exist all the way up and all the way down Reality. They begin at the first nanoseconds of the Big Bang, where in the first equations of physics, we already have attraction and repulsion, as philosopher of science Howard Bloom has pointed out.

- Attraction is a circle quality of *allurement:* moving towards, encircling, creating relationship with communion.
- Repulsion is *autonomy:* independence, the vector. *I am independent, I have my own line, my own direction, my own trajectory, my own plotline, my own story forward.*

Those both exist in Reality, and at some point they *engender* in both men and women, masculine and feminine. But it's not that lines are men and circles are women. Men and women are both lines and circles.

Every man has both line and circle.

Every woman has both line and circle.

Every man and every woman is a unique configuration of lines and circles, this is what we call, in CosmoErotic Humanism, unique gender.[26]

That's the beginning of the vision of *Homo amor: the new human and new humanity.*

This is a very deep read we are doing, and it's very subtle. It's going to get *less* subtle, meaning it's going to get more and more clear—but we're doing an insanely subtle read here, step by step.

We want to create this model in culture of how we read movies as a sacred text of culture.

We are going to deepen this, until we know how to read these texts of culture. Then we are going to explode this into culture. **Because this is where culture gets the storyline wrong, and we need to be able to correct the storyline**.

But first, we have to *see it.*

We want to blow our hearts open here. This is prayer. We are pouring our deepest heart's desire into enacting a new source code and telling a new story. We have to do it for real. Let's just stay in together and do something unimaginably beautiful.

We are going to literally re-weave, together, the source code of consciousness and culture. We're going to do it not by making something go viral, we're going to do it by *thinking clearly together.*

---

26 Ibid., 14. See also: *From Gender Crisis to Unique Gender: The Erotic Cosmos of Lines,Circles, and Spirals* (Gafni, 2025)

CHAPTER 5

"THE UNIVERSE: A LOVE STORY" IN THE MOUTH OF PATRIARCHY

BARBIE LAND: WE HAVE IT ALL WORKED OUT

So, *Barbie* opens with this scene where you see Barbie in a bathing suit, the original doll—and then we are told that Barbie has evolved. As we saw in the previous chapters, Barbie went from being the classical level-one Barbie (a housewife, a beautiful woman raising the family) to integrating the second-wave feminism, claiming of the beautiful and gorgeous and intrinsic role of the feminine in all dimensions of society.

The first wave of feminism is the early suffrage movement, the very first feminists both in Europe and in America in the mid-19th century. The second-wave feminism explodes in the early 60s. Betty Friedan writes *The Feminine Mystique*, and feminism explodes. All of a sudden, Barbie is everything: she's a doctor, and she's a lawyer, and she's a gardener, and she's winning Nobel Prizes, and she's an entrepreneur. **There is this sense that**

now we have equal rights and everything is solved, a utopian sense that we have it all worked out.

That's how the movie opens.

We meet a woman who is called Stereotypical Barbie. She is the protagonist of the movie. She is perfect, she is accomplished, she is smart, she is elegant, she is poised—and **none of that is *for Ken*.** That's just who she is. She is the second-level integrated feminine who has claimed a lot of her potential capacities that had been split off in culture.

And yet, we have the fragrance that she is also stepping out of her relationship to Ken. By "Ken," I mean she is stepping out of the very fact that there is a love story at all, the very fact that *relationship matters*. She is in her own place, and she has it all worked out.

They are all living in Barbie Land. Barbie Land is the world of ideas. It's the world of what I would call *platonic forms*, if you will. Plato has this idea that there is the purified, clarified form, the structure, the clear idea. If you just embody those clarified forms, then everything works out very well. The more you are dissociated or alienated from those forms, the more things break down. But of course, Plato and Barbie Land didn't account for the complexity of the world, the messiness of the world, the contradictions in the world, the experiences in the world that actually can't be dealt with through Plato and the platonic forms.

That's how the movie opens. There is this beautiful scene in the beginning of the movie, where one of Stereotypical Barbie's friends says:

> "Oh, for me, logic and feeling work really well together, and there is no contradiction at all, and my ability to fully experience my feeling doesn't diminish my logic, and my logic doesn't diminish my feeling, they are in complete and perfect balance."

It is an idealized world in which everything fits, and everything is whole, and everything is the way it should be.

LINES AND CIRCLES—ALL THE WAY UP AND DOWN THE EVOLUTIONARY CHAIN

In a previous chapter we introduced a structure called *lines and circles*. **Lines and circles are geometric structures of Reality itself.** Lines and circles are inherent in the structure of Reality, all the way down and all the way up the evolutionary chain.

A scientific way of talking about circle and line might be *attraction* and *repulsion*.

- Attraction: I'm allured towards, I'm drawn towards, I want to be in the circle with you, I want to be drawn towards you, we want to create communion together.
- Repulsion: Get out of my space, I am independent, I am autonomous.

Autonomy and communion, or autonomy and allurement, or repulsion and attraction, are another way of talking about lines and circles.

There are about ten qualities of line and ten qualities of circle, and each quality has a light expression and a shadow expression. Line and circle are phallus and yoni, but phallus and yoni is a human expression (although it started earlier in the mammalian world, but ultimately it gets very distinct in the human world). But lines and circles are an expression of a deeper quality in Cosmos. (Notice that we are both repeating (circle) and deepening (line), forming a spiral.)

- **The quality of line engenders in men.** Not only in men, but there is a particular, intense quality of line that lives within the masculine. At certain moments in time, it gets more intense, and at other times, it's less intense, but there are strong line qualities that live in the masculine. They live in the feminine too but are often more pronounced in the masculine.

- **The quality of circle engenders in the feminine.** Some of that engendering is cultural, and other pieces of that engendering are biological.

In other words:

- Line and circle are qualities of Cosmos, they exist all the way up and all the way down the evolutionary chain—the world of matter, the world of life, and the world of the self-reflective human mind.
- In the human world, they engender in men and women, with a primary engenderment of line qualities in men, and a primary engenderment of circle qualities in women. But all women have line and circle qualities, and all men have line and circle qualities.
- Some of the line and circle qualities in the human realm are purely cultural, pure social constructions, while others are essential qualities that live more essentially in men and women.

Why?

Well, because what we call *gender* is both a social construction and it also has a dimension that's real, that lives inside of men and women. That's why there is a hormonal uniqueness to men and women, and there is an anatomical brain structure unique to men and women. There is a male brain and a female brain; there is a male hormone structure and a female hormone structure—those are both real. There is lactation: women create milk, they have breasts, they breastfeed, they have wombs. They have qualities of nurturance and caring that are uniquely available in that feminine form. Men have greater upper body strength; they don't have the risk of miscarrying during childbirth, because they're not doing childbirth. There are obvious objective essential distinctions—and that's just a starting point.

There is also what we now know as *neuroplasticity*. It means that even anatomical brain structures can gradually shift, transpose, and evolve. While we might begin with a male and female brain, for example, both the male brain and the female brain evolve. The male brain might absorb more and more circle qualities, and the feminine brain might absorb more and more line qualities.

So—

- We have **essential differences between men and women**—there's a different quality to the feminine and masculine. Let's call it Hawaii and New York. Hawaii: feminine, New York: masculine. They are different qualities. Bali and London, they are different qualities. We know those qualities are different, they are the sensual Field of Eros that engenders in these two ways.
- And yet, **there is no sharp distinction**. We are more than just men and women. We are some unique combination of line qualities and circle qualities. We are not just men, we are not just women—we are a Unique Gender, a unique interpenetration of line and circle qualities.

That was a very short summation of a huge piece of the new story of Value, which we are calling *Lines and Circles*.

KEN IS ACTING OUT THE SHADOW OF THE LINE QUALITY

Now, with that in mind, let's look at the scene where Ken is acting out the shadow of the line quality, and he is saying to the other Kens, *I'm going to beach you off.*

What do we see?

The light qualities of line would be:

- Line thrusts forward, the line **competes**.
- You are either higher on the line or lower on the line. Line creates **hierarchy**.
- Line is always: *I am on this side of the line, you are on that side of the line.*

- It **distinguishes**, in very beautiful ways, and analyzes.
- It makes **decisions**.
- It moves **forward**, it's **directional**.

But in its shadow quality it would be drawing a line in the sand, as we see in this scene, just in order to express my desire to distinguish myself from you. It is not a *real* distinction, but a *false* distinction. Not a real *Eros* of distinction, but a false *arbitrary* distinction.

In this scene, we see **Ken acting out the shadow of the line quality**. He is saying, *I'm going to beach off against you.*

Earlier we analyzed the moment right before this scene, where he smashed into the wall. We talked about this in terms of the hero, and the critique, the undermining, the mocking of the very notion of hero.

Now we will look at the shadow of the line quality. Ken is going to have a fight, with this other Ken persona, this other man on the beach. What are they fighting about? Nothing. It's a shadow line quality.

Then the feminine comes in. Barbie separates them. *You absurd dumb men.* She doesn't say it out loud, she smiles. But it's obviously an absurd argument between the Kens. It's an expression of the shadow quality of the line.

By the way, the only person who is unique, the only vague hope for a future is this minor character (like a minor character in Shakespeare), Allan, of whom the narrator says: "There are no multiples of Allan. He's just Allan." There is just one of Allan. Allan is this vague hope for a new possibility that never gets played out in the movie.

THE UNIVERSE: A LOVE STORY IN THE MOUTH OF PATRIARCHY

The theme that runs through the movie is that Ken, at different key points in the movie, says:

I only exist in Barbie's gaze. Only when Barbie looks at me do I exist.

After Ken smashes into the wall mindlessly, trying to attract and allure Barbie's gaze, what's the first thing that he said? He says, "How much of that did you see?" **He needs to be seen in Barbie's gaze.**

Again, the movie mocks that. That's the male expression of the first-level feminine that makes herself beautiful only to be seen in the male gaze. The critique of the male gaze. At level-one feminine, where I dress up to attract the man, to seduce the man, perhaps in order to gain security, or because in some sense, I feel like I don't fully exist outside of the male gaze. There is an enormous feminist literature on interrogating and critiquing the tyranny of the male gaze. That level-one feminine is now transposed to Ken, who is expressing the same shadow of the level-one feminine, but this time on the masculine side.

Is Ken totally wrong?

He is not.

There is the pathological version of codependency, where I can only locate myself in your gaze. That's one pathological version of codependency: I don't exist outside of your gaze.

However it's also true. There is also a beautiful and gorgeous realization that, in some sense, I literally don't exist without your gaze.

I don't exist unless you're placing your gaze on me.

You are the air I breathe, and I flower and I bloom through your gaze.

That's the nature of Eros, and that nature of Eros is not merely a human construction. It's the nature of Reality.

Let's open our hearts, let's dive in deeper.

What the movie is doing is **putting the belief in The Universe: A Love Story in the mouth of patriarchy.** Ken is going to gradually incarnate patriarchy throughout the course of the movie. In the beginning, he's just the shadows or remnants of patriarchy, he's not there yet. But throughout the movie, he's going to incorporate patriarchy in a greater and greater, and more and more dramatic, fashion.

Ken, who's going to later incorporate patriarchy, is expressing the belief in The Universe: A Love Story—but in its pathological form. This is a pathologized version of The Universe: A Love Story.

THE UNIVERSE: A LOVE STORY IN THE NEW PHYSICS

The Universe: A Love Story says, *all of Reality is relationships.* There is no Reality that exists independently of relationships, which means there is no such thing as *a thing.*

If you read Pauli, Plank, Schrödinger—the founders of quantum mechanics—you get this sense that they understand, in a very profound way, that there is no such thing as a thing.

That's what modern physics, the new physics, which is about 100 years old, tells us. Physics has taken many deeper directions, but the ground of the new physics stands, and the ground of the new physics says **there's no such thing as a thing.**

Meaning, the world is not *just matter.* Matter itself is a set of relationships. It's a set of allurements.

We call it matter because we need to give it a name. We call it an atom, a molecule. An atom is the building block of matter, but what *is* an atom?

An atom is a proton and electron allured to each other—an atom is a set of allurements and autonomies. It's a line and circle relationship—because Reality is Eros.

Eros is neither line nor circle. Eros is the unique dance between lines and circles.

Eros exists between protons and electrons, which come together in that relational structure in which they can actually *feel* each other. They can, if you will, *see* each other. They *recognize* each other. There is *intimacy* between subatomic particles.

THE INTIMACY EQUATION APPLIED TO BARBIE AND KEN

Intimacy means something very specific.

Let us start with **the intimacy equation,** which is one of the interior science equations of the new Story of Value:

> Intimacy = shared identity in the context of (relative) otherness, mutuality of recognition, mutuality of pathos (feeling), mutuality of value, and mutuality of purpose.

We create **shared identity**—we don't actually exist without each other. There is mutuality of **recognition**: we recognize each other, we see each other. From seeing each other and recognizing each other, we **feel** each other. We have mutuality of *pathos*. We have a shared **Field of Value** together, and that creates a **shared purpose.**

The realization that Reality is relationship means that, in some sense, the proton and the electron exist fully only in relationship to each other. You can't actually tease them apart. **An atom is this place in which proton and electron gaze on each other, and that gazing, that *mutuality of recognition*, generates the atom.** In a prototypical sense they *feel each other*, and they have *a shared value,* and **their shared value is that they both want to create something new, which is called an atom**. That's their shared value, their shared Eros, which allows them to have a shared *purpose.*

In the actual nature of Reality, Reality is Barbie and Ken.

So, Ken is pointing to something true. He's saying: *no, actually, I don't exist outside of Barbie's gaze.* But in the movie, it's a pathological version of that truth, because he is looking for *fusion* with Barbie before he is *individuated.*

79

Intimacy means *shared identity* in the context of *otherness.* Ken has lost the second part, the otherness: he doesn't have a sense of being Ken. That's one of the things that the movie correctly points to:

- Ken needs to individuate, he needs to become Ken.
- Barbie needs to individuate, she needs to become Barbie.

That's a correct understanding in the movie.

But they need to individuate *in order to create intimacy,* because intimacy means that there is no Barbie without Ken, and there is no Ken without Barbie. And yet, there is not just BarbieKen. There are Barbie *and* Ken who create not *fusion,* BarbieKen, but *union*—Barbie *and* Ken, Ken *and* Barbie—a larger whole.

The movie, paradoxically, gets a dimension of the intimacy equation (intimacy equals shared identity in the context of otherness):

- Ken ignores the otherness.
- Barbie is pure otherness.

For her, Ken is a joke. She is nice to Ken, and she is polite to Ken, but she is mocking Ken. *Oh Ken, you're a beautiful hero, look how beautiful you beach*—but it's not real, as we saw. She is completely alienated and dissociated from any sense that her identity is in any way bound up with Ken. And remember, all the men are named Ken.

She is purely Barbie.

Ken doesn't have a sense of being Ken. Ken has to individuate—but we individuate in order to create a larger union.

The only true individuation is in the context of a larger union.

The only mature individuation is the context of a larger union.

I have to individuate as a Unique Self, but **my uniqueness is not just my being a separate self.** I am a unique expression of this larger field, this larger communion. By individuating uniquely, I can then create, with you, a new, unique, larger union and a new intimacy.

REALITY IS THE EVOLUTION OF RELATIONSHIPS

The movie is mocking the notion that I only exist in your gaze. It is expressing this notion in pathological terms.

- **Level one is the pathological version**. The pathological version is a **fused identity**: *there's no me without you, there's no you without me. There is no me at all.* That can't be true. If I am only I because I am seen by you, and you are only you because you are seen by me, then I am not I and you are not you. There's just fusion. So we need to individuate.

- **Level two is: we individuate.** We say, no, no, we are not fused, we are individuated. I don't want to be fused with you, I want to be in some sort of partnership with you, or I don't need you at all. **I am individuated, I am separate from you.** That's what Barbie is saying: there is no love story, I am just Barbie. There's this realization at level two that intimacy can't just be level-one shared identity, it needs to be level-two intimacy: shared identity in the context of otherness.

But if you read the intimacy equation more clearly, it says: Intimacy = shared identity in the context of (***relative***) otherness.

It's not *absolute* otherness: we are part of the same field. We actually don't exist independently of each other, we don't exist independently of the larger whole, and we don't exist independently of unique relationships that take place within the larger whole.

In other words, Reality is not made up of things. There are no things in Reality. All things are relationships. Reality is, at its core, relationships. That's what Reality is.

1. Reality is relationships.

2. Reality is evolution.
3. Reality is the evolution of relationships.

That's the nature of Reality.

Ken is actually pointing to a truth, but the movie mocks that truth.

What's the truth?

I don't exist independently of your gaze. Without mutuality of recognition between us, there is no me.

Ken gets that, but he gets that in a pathological version. He knows the truth, but he doesn't quite know how to articulate it. He doesn't know how to be Ken, and then say to Barbie: *from that place of being Ken, I'm going to create this shared intimate communion with you.*

He doesn't know how to do that, and Barbie doesn't know how to do that. Neither Ken nor Barbie know how to get to level three, which is **intimate communion in the context of individuated Unique Self: we are Unique Selves coming together forming a unique *we*.** We are intimacy—shared identity in the context of relative otherness. That's real intimacy. They did not get to that yet.

The movie stops at pathologized versions of level two, because that's where culture has stopped.

Before we take the next step, I want to say one more thing. Ken says I'm going to *beach off.*

What does *beach off* sound like? It sounds like I'm going to *beat off.* It's this male masturbatory moment—but not in its beauty. It's not the beauty of a masculine self-pleasuring—because the masculine has lost its own access to the beauty of its self-pleasuring, much like the feminine has.

82

Self-pleasuring is an act of enormous beauty. It is being madly in love with the Field of Reality that lives in you—but that's not available to Ken. *I'm going to beach off*—it has this sense of degradation.

It's this line quality in its shadow form.

It's this desperation to feel alive by drawing an arbitrary line in the sand, which is often what male masturbation becomes. Pornography began as a structure to allow for male masturbation, but not in its beautiful sense, not in the beautiful sense of self-pleasuring. It's just a subtle play in the movie on *beach off* and *beat off* that plays in the background.

KISS IS AT THE VERY HEART OF REALITY AND THE HIJACKING OF "FOREVER"

Now let's go look at the next scene. Remember where Ken reaches out to kiss Barbie, after the dance night?

That is a brutal scene.

Ken tries to kiss Barbie. Why is he trying to kiss Barbie?

Because as the great Christian mystic Meister Eckhart almost said (I'm paraphrasing him), *Reality is kissing itself all the time.* Or, as the interior sciences in Hebrew wisdom say, Reality is *sod ha-nishikin*: it's the secret of the kiss.

> *The secret of the kiss is at the very heart of Reality.*

He leans over to kiss her. Why does he lean over to kiss her? Because he is messed up? Because he is pathological? No! Because **he is The Universe: A Love Story in person.**

Is he leaning over in order to abuse her, to sexually harass her? No, he is *yearning*.

As my dear friend Warren Farrell points out in his writing, the masculine—in the way that culture is structured—risks rejection 500 times for every time the masculine moves towards the feminine. The masculine has to take risk after risk after risk, and he details around twenty-five different moments in which the masculine can be rejected. All of that is encapsulated here, there is incredible vulnerability. He is reaching forward, and what's the look on Barbie's face? *What are you doing?* She is not interested. She is not in the field of allurement—because Barbie is saying, there is no love story.

The movie is pathologizing the sense that there is a love story. We've already pointed out a couple of ways that this happens in the movie. **It is pathologizing the kiss, which is the core of Reality.**

What does Ken say? He says, *could I stay over tonight?* And she says, *why would you stay over?*

There is nothing for us to do.

There is nothing between us.

There is no shared identity.

There is no yearning that's real.

There is no longing that participates in the Field of Eros.

There is no Field of Eros.

There is no field of allurement.

There is no Field of Value.

When you ask ChatGPT—which is an expression of machine intelligence, an oracle summarizing where culture is—**it tells us that value is not real,** and that love as a value is not real. It's a social construction. It's made up. There is no real, ontological truth of The Universe: A Love Story.

What does that mean? There's no "girlfriend and boyfriend." That very structure doesn't actually *exist* for Barbie, other than as an artificial social structure when she says to Ken, in the first scene, *you are so brave*, after he has idiotically smashed into the barrier, in order to obsessively, pathologically gain her gaze, in a tragic sense.

So *Barbie* says:

- A kiss can be part of the polite social convention, but there's no ontology of the kiss.
- There is no ontology of Eros.
- There is no ontology of "girlfriend and boyfriend."

When Ken leans in for a kiss, she says, "You can go now." Who can feel the rejection in that?

She says, "It's girls' night," and then she says, "It's girls' night every night." And then she says, "It's girls' night every night, *forever.*"

Forever is a quality of eternity.

Falling in love means *I am blown away by your beauty, I can't live without you.*

I don't mean falling in love in the romantic sense of we are going to get a U-Haul and move in together. There is a much wider sense of falling in love. I can actually fall in love with 30 people, with 30 men and 30 women. Our love lists are too short, meaning we have a much smaller circle of people that we really fall in love with. Maybe it would be one person, maybe two, maybe three, but there are different levels of falling in love. We were doing a major event in 2014, and our Board Chair then, who has been a dear friend over the years, John Mackey, who founded Whole Foods, turned to me and I turned to John, and we said, *I am in love with you.*

- Falling in love means we have *shared identity in the context of otherness,* for real.
- Falling in love means *I don't have identity without you.*

It's deep, and it's real. There are many different levels of falling in love, but when you really fall in love deeply, you say, *Oh my god, forever, forever!*

Falling in love has a quality of *forever*. And in the movie, *forever* has been hijacked out of a love story. Not intentionally, the writers aren't doing this intentionally; they're not philosophers taking an intentional philosophical stance. Culture speaks unconsciously through the lens of the scriptwriters—they say, girls' night is *forever*.

There is only a narcissistic I, neutered I.

There is no Eros.

There is no girlfriend and boyfriend.

There is no kiss.

BARBIE CANNOT SAY *I LOVE YOU*

As Barbie walks away, what does Ken say? He says, "I love you too." What does *I love you too* mean here? It means Barbie doesn't know how to say *I love you.*

I love you too **is placed in the mouth of this pathological emasculated masculine**—who is *caricaturing* the masculine, not embodying the masculine. All he can say is, *I love you too.* He is a caricatured version—but he's actually reaching for something real.

But she can't say it, it doesn't exist for her. Stereotypical Barbie cannot say *I love you.*

Stereotypical Barbie—in these three levels of the masculine and feminine—is feminine level-two, who has asserted her autonomy and no longer has any sense of needing a man.

At level one—in the healthy forms of level one—there is a sense that men and women *need* each other. There is some polarity between men and women, there is some sense that we are playing different roles and we need each other.

We correctly want to liberate ourselves from the constriction of those roles, so we go to level two. And in the classical level two in culture—I am not talking about the movie now—there is the sense in which women individuate, which is healthy: they break the tyranny of the feminine role at level one. But then they get to this new place, which is, *why do I need a man, what do I need you for?* There is no love story. Wow, that's tragic!

The masculine at level two feels like, *who am I? I knew what it meant to be a hero when I was the primary breadwinner.* But now, in so many houses across the world, the man is not the primary breadwinner; less and less men are primary breadwinners.

What does it mean to be a hero?

Less and less men are heroes in war, thank God—but what does it mean, to be a hero?

Who am I?

When masculine sexuality is demonized, when the essential nature of the masculine is portrayed as inherently brutal by much of second-wave feminism, *I don't even know what it means to be a hero. I am completely lost—so I'm going to be a hero by beaching*—which is this arbitrary mocked version of the hero.

And yet, Ken is holding this longing for the love story.

But Ken's love is reduced. Love, the Eros of Cosmos, is reduced to the failure to individuate and a codependent drive. There is a pathological form of love which is codependency, for sure. But that's not what love is. In other words, **love is reduced to its pathologized form.**

- If you think you only exist in the gaze of love, then you're a pathologically codependent person.
- And, actually, the truth is *we do only exist in the gaze of love.* That's actually true.

The movie is placing that longing in the persona of Ken, who's going to be fundamentally mocked throughout the movie. Ken is never going to be redeemed in this movie. He's going to have certain moments where we have some sympathy for him, but Ken will not be redeemed in this movie.

Doesn't that just break your heart?

CHAPTER 6

DENIAL OF THE AMOROUS COSMOS: FIVE KEY SCENES IN BARBIE SHOWING LOVE IS NOT REAL

The essential point of *Barbie* is that there's only Barbie. There's no Barbie and Ken. The movie ignores the notion that Reality is a love story. It doesn't even come up. The assumption of *Barbie* is that I am a desiccated separate self, that sexuality is not intrinsic to nature in any way, that love, or Barbie and Ken, or LoveDesire, is simply a social construction. That's the assumption of *Barbie*.

There are at least five moments in *Barbie* that all point to that in a different way. We've briefly mentioned all of them. In this chapter, we're going to recapitulate and deepen the five key scenes that deny that the Universe is a love story.

SCENE ONE: "I ONLY EXIST IN YOUR GAZE"

Ken Only Has a Great Day When Barbie Looks at Him

The movie opens with the voice-over saying, "Barbie has a great day every day. Ken only has a great day when Barbie looks at him." That's a theme we've talked about.

Where else does this theme appear?

So, that appears again, later in the movie when Barbie has come back to Barbie Land after the trip to the real world, and Ken has taken over Barbie Land with the guys. The women are in some sort of regressive trance, serving the men in a disempowered way. **Barbie, together with Gloria, Sasha and other women burst the women out of this regressive trance through the feminist speech.** They decide they're going to change the constitution, and they're going to take back Barbie Land. They succeed in doing it because the men who are considered idiots, always forget how to do proper strategies—they're portrayed as idiots.

There's this conversation between Barbie and Ken, which is a very poignant conversation, in which Ken says to Barbie, "I thought this would be our house." They have this very beautiful conversation. In that conversation, Ken says, *I only feel good in the warmth of your gaze.*

Ken actually owns it himself, "I only feel good within the warmth of your gaze."

What is Ken saying? He says that Reality is a love story. If Reality is a love story, then I can have a great job, I can have my family, and all sorts of love in my family, but if I don't have a particular quality of a living love story, then something is missing. I'm not quite alive. **Unless I live in the warmth of your gaze, I don't feel fully alive. That's what a love story means.** If Reality is a love story, then if I'm not in a love story. I don't feel fully alive. Or if my love story is not fully alive, then I don't feel fully alive.

In other words, my love story is not an extra. My love story is the currency and quality of Reality itself. **If I'm feeling alive and awake in my love story, I feel at home in the Universe.** Then I'm having, like Ken in Barbie's gaze, *a great day.*

Let's just check if this is true. Of course, it's true. Anyone who has a daughter, son, friend, parent, or beloved that you've interacted with and had a huge fight with knows it's true. Because how has the rest of your day gone? Not too well. Why? You didn't lose your house, you didn't lose your car, you didn't lose your job, but you feel like shit. Why do you feel terrible? You feel terrible because there's some clash between you and this one person. It could be a close friend. It could be a family member. There are many forms of Outrageous Love, but these close relationships, they are an expression of what we call The Universe: A Love Story.

- When a close relationship is challenged, when it's broken, then I feel something is broken in The Universe: A Love Story.
- We are incarnations of The Universe: A Love Story.
- Our relationships are The Universe: A Love Story in person.
- We are CosmoErotic Humanism in person.

That's what we are. So when I'm wildly aflame and in love, or I'm quietly tender and in love, then I'm at home in the Universe, because the Universe is a love story.

Therapy is wrong when it says, "You can't let anyone define how you feel." This is the classical line in the human potential movement: "You feel bad? That's your own responsibility. No one can make you feel bad." That's nonsense. Of course someone else can make you feel bad. The Universe is a love story. The notion that somebody else can't make you feel bad means that there's only one value in the Cosmos, which is autonomy, meaning individual parts, a Cartesian world, in which you're an individual separate part. You have integrity. You feel good. Why would you let anyone else enter your world and rob from you the autonomy and self-authority over your own mood? This is what various forms of human potential therapy tell us all the time.

Now it's not that this is completely wrong. It's true, but partial. Meaning, you don't want to let just anyone hijack your mood. You want to have some self-love. You want to have some self-love and some authority over your own interior. That's of course true. But of course someone else who you love can step in and ruin your mood. Of course they can. You can recover it afterwards, but **if there's no one who can ruin your mood, that means you're not alive.** It means you don't care for anyone. It means you're not in love with anyone.

So Reality is a love story.

That's why I'm at home in the Universe when I'm in love.

That's beautiful.

That's what Ken says to Barbie.

But Ken is mocked as a *fucking* idiot for saying that, meaning, **the love story is placed in the mouth of patriarchy.**

It's very, very powerful.

What the movie does implicitly, not intentionally, is that it says, *Ken is patriarchy, and patriarchy is what Ken does.* There's a big part of Ken which loves patriarchy.

But who's the person that actually experiences the love story?

Ken the idiot or Ken patriarchy, one of the two, is the person who's **championing The Universe: A Love Story.**

In the movie, love is only a social construction. This is the classical post-modern desiccation of story and of value. Story is not real. Love is not real. Value is not real, meaning Eros is not a value of Cosmos. It's not actually real.

Who tries to make it real? Patriarchy. Why? Because **love becomes a form of power.** It's my form of power over you. The breaking out of that form of power, in order to establish that Barbie is fully autonomous, is the move that *Barbie* wants to make.

That move is exactly half true. What's true is that Barbie shouldn't be defined *entirely*, nor should Ken, by their relationship.

My love story, my set of relationships is a *dimension* of my life. Intimate communion is a dimension of Reality, but **one dimension of this intimate communion is actually my *autonomy.***

Intimate communion doesn't mean that I have fused with you. It means,

- I have autonomy.
- I have individual integrity.
- We're in intimate communion.
- We're not using each other.
- We're not exclusively defined in terms of each other.
- We're not codependent in an inappropriate way.
- I need some sense of not just being Mrs. X, I'm also Barbie.

That's beautiful.

The rebellion against Barbie being defined exclusively by her relationship, or Ken being defined exclusively by his relationship, is itself an evolution of consciousness, which is an evolution of love.

But that's not what the movie's doing. The movie does that *in part*, but then it goes the next step and says *there's no Ken and Barbie* and *there is no love story.*

SCENE TWO: KEN'S SONG "I HAVE FEELINGS I CAN'T EXPLAIN"

The only person in the movie who claims that *LoveDesire* is real is Ken. In the "I'm Just Ken," where Ken talks about the feeling of desire—the feeling of *LoveDesire*—he is portrayed as wrong.

In the song, Ken says,

> *I have feelings I can't explain. They're driving me insane.*
> *Where I see love, she sees a friend.*
>
> *What will it take for her to see the man behind the tan and fight for me?*
>
> *I wanna know what it's like to love, to be the real thing.*
> *Is it a crime?*
>
> *Am I not hot when I'm in my feelings?*
> *Is my moment finally here or am I dreaming?*

Ken is standing for desire and the dignity of desire and for the *LoveEros* of Cosmos, but the movie mocks it because Ken is patriarchy who's a blithering idiot. That's the point. So the first point we're making here is this: **the entire notion that there is a love story is placed in Ken's mouth and is rejected as the idiocy of patriarchy.**

Let's take a deeper look at the Ken song.

There's a song that Ken sings, it's an incredible scene in the movie where all the Kens are fighting each other on the beach.

- Step one, Ken in the movie stands for love. He's standing for the notion that *love is real.*
- Step two, the insidious move that the movie is making is Ken is patriarchy, so **that which stands for *love is real* is patriarchy.**

Patriarchy is saying *love is real*, but it's a strategy of patriarchy. That's the point the movie is making. All the reviews just missed it or ignored it. It's blatant.

Now, let's take a look at the lyrics. Let's just read the text. These are the first two lines of the song:

> *Doesn't seem to matter what I do.*
> *I'm always number two.*

It starts with caricaturing the male as someone who is, in rivalrous conflict governed by win/lose metrics, always number two. The entire fight scene on the beach is a caricature of male violence.

If you look at the opening scene of the movie *Saving Private Ryan*, guys are mowed down on the beach. This too is a beach scene, men fighting on the beach. But of course, the beach is a place where men have died. Millions of men died on beaches.

But what does Ken say? I just want you to catch the resonance: *I beach*. And what is *beaching*?

This *beaching* is this great war between men, and it's a war—if you remember the plotline of the movie—over perceived egoic insults from the feminine. We men feel slighted, so we actually create a war over those trifling contraction insults. This is what is meant with men who are *beaching*: male violence is caricatured as inanely stupid on the beach. But then the lyrics of the Ken song during this scene are (and it's shocking):

> *Doesn't seem to matter what I do.*
> *I'm always number two.*
> *No one knows how hard I tried. Oh, oh.*

These are the first three lines of the song "I'm Just Ken." Now take a look at the fourth line. This fourth line is mocked in the movie. It's easy to miss it and not even catch it. Take a look at the fourth line:

> *I have feelings I can't explain.*

But those feelings, as they are explained by the movie, are just the social construction of a sick patriarchy. But what Ken is saying is—and this is where the Goddess finds Her way to speak through the lyrics:

> *I have feelings I can't explain.*
> *They're driving me insane.*
> *All my life's become so polite.*
> *But I'll sleep alone tonight.*

Critics read it: the guy always needs a babe in his bed. But that's actually not what he's saying.

Despite the critics' best efforts, the Goddess found her way here.

> *I have feelings I can't explain.*

How do I know what I know? Anthro-ontology, human ontology, meaning: it lives in me, the mysteries are within us. *I have feelings I can't explain. They're driving me insane.*

The normal consciousness of evolutionary psychology of win/lose metrics is that I'm supposed to be completely satisfied in the polite place. *All my life I've been so polite. I've operated in that system, it's driving me insane. And I'll sleep alone tonight.*

And then the next line. Why?

> *Because I'm just Ken.*
> *I'm just Ken,*
> *Anywhere else, I'd be a ten.*

Then he reverts back. There are multiple voices of I'm just Ken: I got it. Let me push that feeling down. I'm just Ken. Got it. Patriarchy.

He reverts back into the other voice. As my friend Dick Schwartz described in Internal Family Systems, there are different voices that live in us. We see Ken's different voices here.

And then he says this incredible line. It's really beautiful that he says this gorgeous line, he says:

Is it my destiny to live and die a life of blond fragility?

Isn't that a gorgeous line? And they wrote it cutely, slapstick, but *She—the Goddess*—found her way into the line. *Is it my destiny to live and die a life of blond fragility?* Shakespeare couldn't have done that much better. It's a gorgeous line, but it gets completely lost, it hasn't been commented on by anyone. *Is it my destiny?* And then he says, *I'm just Ken.* Here's the next key line:

Where I see love, she sees a friend.

But he's not just talking about their relationship. He is actually saying, where he holds the possibility of the Universe as a love story, she is saying love as a value is not real.

Then he says:

What will it take for her to see the man behind the tan and fight for me?

Is that just male ego? There's some male ego there for sure. But is that male ego *at its core*? No. *What will it take for her to see the man behind the tan?*

Now, does he have a huge responsibility in the level of superficiality—a responsibility to be more than the guy with the tan? Of course he does. That's a given. The opposite of the sacred is the superficial. That's a given. We get the critique of Ken, that's a good critique. It's a good critique of patriarchy. Received.

But he is saying something here. He's saying, *I want her to see me. I'm actually desperate for her to see me. What will it take for her to see the man behind the tan and fight for me?*

You have to understand, these are the lyrics to that scene on the beach, that caricatured scene on the beach. These are the actual lyrics to that, which many people don't quite catch.

And then he says:

> *I want to know what it's like to love, to be the real thing.*
> *Is it a crime?*

Is it some violation? What am I doing wrong here? What he's saying is, actually: *What everyone is telling me is there is no Barbie and Ken.* It's what Barbie is saying. It's what culture is saying. *I am just Ken.* That's the name of the song, *I'm just Ken.*

Then he says:

> *Am I not hot when I'm in my feelings?*

Can I trust my feelings? All of culture is telling me I can't trust my feelings.

Now I want you to get it really clear, friends. I take the feminist critique of patriarchy in the movie as a given and assume it to be correct. There's obviously a huge critique of patriarchy. I think we can all take it as a given that there was something to critique in patriarchy, and that feminism did a good job of critiquing part of it. That's a given. That's our structure. We're starting from there.

But that's not what the movie is doing.

What it's saying is: *There is no Barbie and Ken.*

> *Is my moment finally here or am I dreaming?*
> *I'm no dreamer.*
>
> *Can you feel KENergy?*
> *Feels so real, my KENergy.*

But then he realizes:

No, I'm just Ken.
Anywhere else, I'd be a ten.
Where I see love, she sees a friend.

And then there is resignation at the end of the song, complete resignation. He says:

I'm just Ken,
And I'm enough.
And I'm great at doing stuff.

Wow. This is complete resignation.

So, hey, check me out, yeah, I'm just Ken.
My name's Ken, and so am I.
Put that manly hand in mine.
So, hey world, check me out, yeah I'm just Ken.
Baby, I'm just Ken.

That's a suicide note. Do you get that? That this was *written* is not the problem. The problem is that this was written and completely *missed* by culture—when actually it's a complete indictment of the very notion of Barbie and Ken.

If Ken would actually mature and wake up, he would awaken to love, but he doesn't. His "waking up" is the realization that love is not real, that there is no Barbie and Ken.

Now, this is not me reading you a postmodern text from Derrida or early Foucault. I am reading you the text that's at the center of culture now. No one bothered to read the song. The critics who did read the song, read it as a male ego song. That's how they read it.

It's not a male ego song. **This is a plaintive cry of a human soul.** It's not a male issue. It's now a man/woman issue. It's *the line*, whoever the line is, this is the line saying, *Oh my god, love is real. And I want her, I want him, to see behind the tan and be willing to fight for me. But where I see love, she sees a friend—I can't trust my feelings.*

The surest way to control you—whether through overt Orwellian totalitarianism as in *1984*, as in a closed society like China, or through open society totalitarianism, as described by B.F. Skinner in *Walden Two* or practiced by the MIT Media Lab—**is to convince you that you can't trust your own feelings.** If you can't trust your deepest feelings—if I can split your own trust of your feelings—I've got you. Wow.

Here's the crazy thing: **There are no demons in the story.** If I brought Alex Pentland into this room, and the entire staff of the MIT Media Lab, you would not meet people with horns. You'd meet fantastic people who you'd love to have dinner with, who you might want to sleep with. Great people, great men and women are running these things.

Existential risk does not come from a conspiracy theory. **There is no conspiracy theory. It's the structure of the system itself.** It's an inexorable movement of the system itself. That's actually what's happening.

SCENE THREE: "WHY WOULD YOU STAY OVER? IT'S GIRLS' NIGHT EVERY NIGHT!"

The next scene we've already discussed, so we will only briefly mention it here. In this scene, the notion of a love story is again with Ken. He wants to stay over with Barbie, and Barbie says, "Why would you stay over?" He moves to kiss her, and Barbie says, "What are you doing?" She says, "It's girls' night, every night, forever!" There's no place for Ken to stay over and Ken is devastated.

He walks away and says under his breath, "I love you too..." He feels this love story, but Barbie has no access to it. The individual kiss is rejected, the notion of kissing, the notion of staying over, the notion of LoveDesire is utterly rejected and is mocked. The love story has been completely undermined.

SCENE FOUR: "YOU'RE JUST KEN"

Scene four, when the dialogue that takes place between Barbie and Ken, when the women reshape the constitution of Barbie Land and there's this conversation where Barbie says to Ken, *You have to realize that you're just Ken.* Ken says something like, *What do you mean I'm just Ken? I'm Ken in relationship to Barbie.* That's the essence of the conversation. And Barbie says something like, *You're not in relationship to me. You're just Ken. There is no Barbie and Ken.*

This is Barbie and Ken after patriarchy collapses. Ken is sobbing and says to Barbie, "I always thought this would be our house." Barbie says, "I think I owe you an apology. I'm sorry I took you for granted." Barbie says, "Not every night had to be girls' night."

So Ken thinks there's an opening to relationship, to the love story. So he leans over to kiss her and she rejects him and he slaps himself. He's like the sexual harasser slapping himself, because why would you lean over to kiss someone?

She says, *What are you doing? Are you out of your mind? I didn't mean to suggest...*

Barbie says, "Maybe it's time to discover who Ken is."

Ken: "I just don't know who I am without you."

Barbie: "You're Ken."

Ken: "But it's 'Barbie and Ken.' There is no 'just Ken.' That's why I was created."

> Ken: "I only exist in the warmth of your gaze. Without it, I'm just another blond guy who can't do flips."

Ken says, "I just don't know who I am without you. It's *Barbie and Ken*. There is no 'just Ken.' That's why I was created." And Ken is right. But Barbie thinks that's ridiculous. *That's not why you're created.* So Barbie says, "Ken, you have to figure out who you are without me."

Ken tries to say, "Oh, Ken is me, Ken is me." He tries to have the sense of, "Wow! I'm just Ken."

But then he gets honest and says, "I don't even care about Ken being Ken anymore. I just miss my friend Barbie. I only exist in Barbie's gaze." But it's mocked again.

SCENE FIVE: BARBIE TELLS RUTH HANDLER, "I AM NOT IN LOVE WITH KEN"

Finally, the fifth scene, is at the very end of the movie, where Sasha, the daughter of Gloria, says, "What about Barbie? What's her ending? What does she get?" The head of Mattel says, "That's easy, she's in love with Ken!" But Barbie says, "I'm not in love with Ken." That's the fifth scene.

To read the movie, you have to gather all five of those scenes and put them together.

We have to read it carefully, not as what we would *like* this movie to say, but as what the movie is actually saying. What we would like the movie to say is that Barbie's saying to Ken, "Why don't you individuate? Become Ken and then come back, then we can get together." That's what we would like the movie to be saying. And that's what the critics who had any sensitivity at all said that's what the movie says, *but it doesn't.*

It's *not* what the movie says.

If you read the scene superficially, it *looks* like she says, "I don't love *this guy*." But that's not what the scene means. She means, *Barbie is not in love with Ken.* She's saying, *Barbie is not in love with Ken; Ken is not in love with Barbie.* **Meaning, love is not the goal.** That's not the ending. *I'm not in love with Ken.* The very structure of "Barbie and Ken" actually doesn't exist. What the movie says is that **there is no "Barbie and Ken." There is no Universe: A Love Story.**

In other words, it's not that *this* Barbie doesn't love *this* Ken. Barbie is a doll and Ken is a doll. What does a doll mean? **It means they're archetypes.** That's what it means. A doll means it's an archetype. It's an archetype of consciousness. **This is the feminine and the masculine.**

There is no love story.

That's the point.

CHAPTER 7

THE EXILE OF THE LOVE STORY & THE DEMONIZATION OF LOVEDESIRE

BARBIE IN THE REAL WORLD

Let's look again at the scene where Weird Barbie tells Stereotypical Barbie to go to the real world. One day Barbie wakes up and she has flat feet, cellulite, and irrepressible thoughts of death. Those are the three reasons that cause Stereotypical Barbie to come to Weird Barbie to ask what to do. Weird Barbie is the jester in King Lear's court. Weird Barbie explains to Barbie that someone in the real world played with Barbie too hard and somehow penetrated the Barbie world with her irrepressible thoughts of death.

So Barbie has to go to the real world to find the woman who had thoughts that connected Barbie to the real world, and fix her. She asked Weird Barbie, "How will I know who that person is?" And Weird Barbie says, "You'll know."

What does Barbie find in the real world?

THE GODDESS APPEARS, BUT WITHOUT DESIRE

There's a moment in the real world where Barbie is sitting on a bench next to an old woman. This old woman is astonishingly beautiful. Barbie says to her, "You're so beautiful." The woman says, "I know." Then Barbie begins to cry these beautiful tears. When she walks away to continue her quest, to look for whoever caused these thoughts, she looks behind at the woman, and she's just blown open in tears. This is a Goddess moment. That old woman, she's the Goddess. That Goddess is pure femininity. Pure *She*. A pure Goddess.

However, **the movie retains this notion of the beauty of the feminine without desire.**

Between Barbie and the old woman, there's no Field of Desire. So Barbie looks at this old woman and she's blown away by her beauty, and she cries these beautiful tears of radiance and ecstasy, because **there is pure love without desire.**

On the one hand, it's a beautiful scene. Barbie's heart is blown open in devotion to the Goddess.

On the other hand, **the Goddess is denuded of desire.**

"ME AND KEN, WE HAVE NO GENITALS"

Remember the scene when Barbie and Ken (who came with her) get to the real world, there are these construction workers that make fun of her, that kind of catcall her. She goes over to the construction workers, and she says, "Basically, me and Ken, we don't have genitals."

Barbie says,

> *I don't know exactly what you meant with all of those little quips, but I'm picking up on some sort of entendre, which appears to be double, and I would just like to inform you, I do not have a vagina—and he does not have a penis.* **We don't have genitals.**

The construction workers are like, "What's wrong with her?" She says, "Why are you guys calling us?" She feels some violence. She doesn't understand the desire. Barbie says, "We don't have genitals. Me and Ken, we have no genitals." **There's no sense of desire. Again, desire is denuded.**

WEIRD BARBIE LOVES "THAT NUDE BLOB UNDER HIS PANTS"

Who has an appreciation of desire in the story early on? Weird Barbie. When Stereotypical Barbie goes to Weird Barbie, Weird Barbie says about Ken, "That Ken of yours, he is one nice-looking little protein pot. I'd like to see what kind of nude blob he's packing under those pants." That's her exact phrase. Not an eloquent phrase, I admit. But the point is that she's pointing to the beauty of the masculine phallus.

Barbie tells us that Ken doesn't even have genitals (although he says he does), but **Weird Barbie actually imagines the phallus. She's holding a devotional imagination of the phallus that no one else in the movie is holding.** She refers to *the nude blob under Ken's pants.*

Weird Barbie feels some phallic quality in Ken, but Barbie doesn't even know what she's talking about.

WEIRD BARBIE UNDERSTANDS WHAT "I LOVE YOU" MEANS

So this notion of allurement to the masculine and some field of phallic presence and desire is only present in Weird Barbie.

Then, when Barbie leaves Weird Barbie to go on her journey, what does Weird Barbie say to her?

"I love you."

But Barbie doesn't understand "I love you."

Ken understands "I love you" in the beginning of the movie. But he's representing patriarchy.

Then later, Weird Barbie, the peripheral figure, says "I love you" to Barbie.

But Barbie doesn't get it.

Weird Barbie has a sense of the dignity of desire in relationship to Ken that Barbie doesn't have.

So when Barbie gets to the real world and sees the construction workers, and she says, "We have no genitals," she means, *What are you guys doing? You guys are weird.*

THE MOTHER-DAUGHTER LOVE STORY IS THE MOVIE'S ONLY REAL LOVE STORY

So where *does* the love story play for Barbie? The love story in the movie is between women. There are several woman-on-woman love stories in the movie. These are primarily love stories between mother and daughter, which take place in several ways.

First, Barbie has a conversation with Ruth Handler, who is the creator of the Barbie dolls, where she says, "Oh, I named you Barbie after my daughter Barbara." So you see kind of a mother-daughter relationship there. **So the big love story is between Ruth and her daughter, Barbara.**

Second, there's the old woman and Barbie on the bench, which we mentioned before.

Third, there's the relationship between Ruth and Barbie. They have two dramatic scenes.

- The first scene is when Barbie is escaping, and the men, who are the board of Mattel, are trying to put her back in the box. As she is escaping, she has this great conversation with Ruth.
- The second scene takes place at the end of the movie, when Barbie wants to become human and Ruth warns her what this would mean.

The **fourth** woman-on-woman love story is the big relationship between the biological mother and daughter, between Gloria and Sasha.

Throughout the movie, there are five or six "Sasha and Gloria fall in love" scenes. Most people don't even notice there's this love story happening. It's a very beautiful love story, between mother and daughter.

The movie can't actually claim that there's no love story at all, but it does say that the love story is basically biological or at least that it's only between women. It's not between women in the sense of beautiful, woman-on-woman *desire*. It's not that kind of relationship between women. It's specifically either mother and daughter, or it's Barbie with the old woman.

It's not a kind of valorization of the beauty of woman-on-woman love. No, it's something else. It's woman-love where *there's no desire*—or there's no desire that is in any way socially accepted. It's between an older woman and a younger woman, or between a mother and daughter. That's where the love story happens.

So there is essentially Agape without Eros, which is the same move that *Star Wars* makes. It basically says, *love exists as Agape, but Eros is rejected.*

So what *Barbie* is saying is that:

- Eros is rejected as a value.
- Agape is the only kind of love that's real.

Suddenly you have the Christian notion of Agape and its rejection of Eros finding its way in *Barbie*.

If we put all the different mother-daughter scenes together, we see **this mother-daughter love story. It's quite beautiful**. One of the high points is when they're in the car and the daughter starts singing with the mother, "I went to the mountain." And there's this moment where they recognize each other. **There's this gorgeous and stunning and beautiful emergence between them.** So in the movie, there's room for that biological mother-daughter love story and it's very beautiful. The mother is slowly seen by her daughter and she loves her perception.

At one key moment, Sasha, the daughter says to Gloria, the mother, "Oh my god! Your drawings are beautiful, and they're stunning." She becomes proud of her mother in this kind of ongoing saga. They influence each other, and there's an insanely beautiful bond of sisterhood between mother and daughter.

First it starts as mother and daughter, and then it moves to a kind of sisterhood. It's just a stunning story.

So, the love story never completely disappears in the movie. It's a moving love story, a notion of feminine empowerment, and a notion of sisterhood.

It's stunning and gorgeous and absolutely valid.

And also:

- It's an exile of love to a love story without desire.
- It's an implicit demonization of LoveDesire.
- It's a complex moment in this **de-eroticized story.**

Barbie is trying to do love without desire, which doesn't work. There's this **attempt to split love and desire.**

And we also don't have a gay love story—Barbie stays strictly heterosexual. The movie ignores the LGBTQ+ community, but that's not our point.

The point is there's no erotic love at all in *Barbie*. But it's even way more dramatic than that. If that was the truth, it'd be utterly uninteresting, but it's actually much, much *more* interesting.

The point of Barbie is not only that there is no erotic love, but that there is no love story in the Universe, which is actually the nature of Cosmos.

You have biological love—you can occasionally have this miracle of women loving each other. There's this unique family moment, which is kind of a sisterly love. You can have mother-daughter love, but **you do not have desire, *Fuck*, or a love story in Cosmos.**

There is no *Fuck* in Cosmos.

Reality is not *Fuck*.

Reality is not Eros.

There is no LoveDesire in Cosmos. It's not real.

What is the word in the movie for LoveDesire in Cosmos?

"Barbie and Ken."

Barbie and Ken are not people, they're archetypes.

It's not about *this* Barbie and *this* Ken, this guy and this girl, that's not what the movie's about.

It's about Barbie and Ken as archetypes of LoveDesire as a core structure in Cosmos, which is utterly destroyed.

CHAPTER 8

THE EVOLUTION OF LOVEDESIRE IN BARBIE SONGS BETWEEN 1997 AND 2023

COMPARING TWO IN BARBIE SONGS

We talked about the demonization of the masculine in Barbie, by looking at how the love story is put in the mouth of patriarchy and how male heroism is utterly mocked. So we want to look at one more thing.

Let's look at two more Barbie songs. I want you to get both the beautiful rebellion and the sad desiccation in this Barbie movie. It's always in the text. You have to read text carefully. Text matters.

When you watch a movie, one of the keys in watching a movie is to listen to the songs. See where they're played. Read the words. Read the texts.

My suggestion is, pick at least two or three movies a year. Just go online and get the actual text of the movie. Just read the text. What's the movie saying? Read the lyrics of the songs. **That's how you begin to listen to culture, but you have to read slowly.** Slowly. I read crazy slow. Everyone assumes I read really fast. I read a lot, but I read extremely slowly. I read word for word for word. There's no cheap grace.

Then you start hearing Goddess talk and kind of share her agenda. In other words, you're not relying on a cultural critic.

Part of being *Homo amor* is to do sensemaking. This is an essential part of *Homo amor*.

THE 1997 BARBIE SONG

So I want to take a look at two Barbie songs. We're going to take a look at the words of the first Barbie song. **This is the 1997 Barbie song.**

1997 Barbie Song Lyrics

Hiya Barbie
Hi Ken!

Do you want to go for a ride?
Sure Ken.
Jump in.

I'm a Barbie girl, in a Barbie world
Life in plastic, it's fantastic.
You can brush my hair, undress me everywhere.
Imagination, life is your creation.

Come on Barbie, let's go party!

I'm a Barbie girl, in a Barbie world
Life in plastic, it's fantastic.
You can brush my hair, undress me everywhere.
Imagination, life is your creation.

I'm a blond bimbo girl, in a fantasy world,
Dress me up, make it tight, I'm your dolly.
You're my doll, rock'n'roll, feel the glamor in pink,
Kiss me here, touch me there, hanky panky.

You can touch,
you can play,
if you say "I'm always yours."
I'm a Barbie girl, in a Barbie World
Life in plastic, it's fantastic.
You can brush my hair, undress me everywhere.
Imagination, life is your creation.

Come on Barbie, let's go party! (Ah ah ah yeah)
Come on Barbie, let's go party! (Oh oh)
Come on Barbie, let's go party! (Ah ah ah yeah)
Come on Barbie, let's go party! (Oh oh)

Make me walk, make me talk, do whatever you please,
I can act like a star, I can beg on my knees.
Come jump in, bimbo friend, let us do it again,
Hit the town, fool around, let's go party.

You can touch,
You can play,
If you say "I'm always yours."
You can touch,
You can play,
If you say "I'm always yours."

Oh, I'm having so much fun!

Well Barbie, we are just getting started.

Oh, I love you Ken.

So that's an incredible song. Let's look at these words, this is 1997. Does everyone get what's happening here? These words are horrific! Just to be clear. **These words are the basic view of the feminine and masculine through the eyes of a very aggressive victim feminism, which is partially right in its critique of the masculine. It's not that it's wrong. It's *partially* right.**

This is the moment of Catharine MacKinnon, who's a legal scholar from the University of Michigan, a brilliant writer. It's the moment of Andrea Dworkin. MacKinnon and Dworkin are critiquing this notion of a kind of male entitlement, which is both delightful and fun and wild and crazy and can also yield towards an intense and inappropriate objectification, dancing with the beauty of objectification.

It's this very complicated, strange song.

So I want to actually look at the lyrics with you. Feel the energy of the song. **The song has a lot of Eros. It has a lot of energy. It has a lot of movement.**

But listen to the words:

> *Hiya Barbie. Hiya Ken. You want to go for a ride? Sure, Ken, jump in.*

> *I'm a Barbie girl in a Barbie World. Life in plastic, it's fantastic. You can brush my hair, undress me anywhere. Imagination, life is your creation.*

So basically, *I'm yours. I am the ultimate woman. I am gorgeous. I am beautiful. Brush my hair, undress me anywhere.* Ken is excited, Barbie's excited. **Everyone's happy in this kind of idealized, beautiful, sexual world, playing without any shame.**

It's this kind of **idealized, strange Garden of Eden.**

Of course, the person who's the object is Barbie. So we're not addressing Ken as an object of desire anywhere. I just want to note that.

So there's a particular kind of vision of the story:

Barbie: *"Imagination, life is your creation. I'm a blonde bimbo girl in a fantasy world. Dress me up. Make it tight, I'm your dolly."*

Ken: *"You're my doll, rock and roll. Feel the glamour in the pink."*

Barbie: *"Kiss me here, touch me there, hanky panky, you can touch, you can play, if you say, I'm always yours."*

The exchange is, if you say I'm always yours, then I give myself to you and you own me.

Remember, this is level-one femininity, where Barbie seduces Ken in exchange for safety and security.

Now is that wrong? No, it's not wrong, but it's partial, it's one-sided. It makes the masculine the owner, not the feminine. It embraces the bimbo, quite literally in the song. *Undress me anywhere*, but only on the Barbie side, not on the Ken side. Yet it has some Eros. It has some aliveness. So, this is the song in 1997.

Let's keep reading.

Barbie: *"Dress me up, make it tight. I'm your dolly. You can touch. You can play if you say, I'm always yours."*

Ken: *"Come on, Barbie. Let's go party."*

Barbie: *"Make me walk, make me talk, do whatever you please. I can act like a star. I can beg on my knees."*

It's 1997 and culture explodes with this Barbie song, which is **both the delight, the Eros, the *Fuck*, and the brokenness, the incompleteness, and the avoiding of the shame.**

It is this confused moment in culture.

Barbie: *"You can touch, you can play, if you say, I'm always yours. Oh, I love you, Ken."*

So there is an "I love you" as the song ends.

There is an "I love you."

There's a Barbie and Ken "I love you."

There is complete Eros and desire.

But the price for owning me is to say, *I'm always yours.*

So this is what the new Barbie franchise 25 years later is rebelling against. The new Barbie franchise says, *fuck that, man, really?* But it does it in a very subtle, complex way.

THE 2023 BARBIE SONG

Now let's look at the new Barbie song that Nicki Minaj and Ice Spice wrote for the 2023 film, sampling the 1997 version.

This is culture responding.

2023 Barbie Song Lyrics

I'm always yours (stop playin' with 'em, RIOT)
Ooh whoa

And I'm bad like the Barbie (Barbie)
I'm a doll, but I still wanna party (party)
Pink 'Vette like I'm ready to bend (bend)
I'm a ten, so I pull in a Ken
Like Jazzie, Stacie, Nicki (grrah)
All of the Barbies is pretty (damn)
All of the Barbies is bad
It girls (it girls) and we ain't playin' tag (grrah)

Rad (rad), but he spank me when I get bad
I'm in LA, Rodeo Drive (Drive)
I'm in New York, Madison Ave
I'm a Barbie girl (girl), Pink Barbie Dreamhouse
The way Ken be killin' shit, got me yellin' out like the Scream

house (woo)
Yellin' out, we ain't sellin' out
We got money, but we ain't lendin' out
We got bars, but we ain't bailin' out
In that pink Ferrari, we peelin' out
I told Tae bring the Bob Dylan out
That pussy so cold, we just chillin' out
They be yellin', yellin', ye-yellin' out
It's Barbie, bitch, if you still in doubt (ooh)

And I'm bad like the Barbie (Barbie)
I'm a doll, but I still wanna party (party)
Pink 'Vette like I'm ready to bend (bend)
I'm a ten, so I pull in a Ken
Like Jazzie, Stacie, Nicki (grrah)
All of the Barbies is pretty (damn)
All of the Barbies is bad
It girls (it girls) and we ain't playin' tag (grrah)

Barbie ain't nothin' to play 'bout
He wanna play in the playhouse (playhouse)
The fuck they gon' say now? (Grrah)
I'm washin' these bitches, I'm rubbin' the stain out
Like I'm ready to bend (grrah)
All the fake Barbies just wanna pretend (like)
Like hold on, let me go find me a pen (grrah)
Look where it led, now I'ma put it to bed
She a Barbie bitch with her Barbie clique (grrah)
I keep draggin' her, so she bald a bit (damn)
And I see the bread, I want all of it (damn)
And I want the green, so I olive it (grrah)
And I throw it back, so he losin' it (like)
And I give the box with no shoes in it (damn)

Yeah, I know the trick, so I got him bricked (damn)
Yeah, they know who lit, me and Barbie, bitch

And I'm bad like the Barbie (Barbie)
I'm a doll, but I still wanna party (party)
Pink 'Vette like I'm ready to bend (bend)
I'm a ten, so I pull in a Ken
Like Jazzie, Stacie, Nicki (grrah)
All of the Barbies is pretty (damn)
All of the Barbies is bad
It girls (it girls) and we ain't playin' tag (grrah)

I'm a Barbie girl in the Barbie world
Life in plastic, it's fantastic
You can brush my hair, undress me everywhere
Imagination

So do we get a taste of that song? If you can, listen to the songs and feel the difference between the two songs. Listen to the lyrics of this second Barbie song in 2023.

"So I'm always yours. Stop playing with them. Riot. Oh, whoa!"

So "I'm always yours" opens the song, but that's a joke. "I'm always yours" is not true.

"Oh, whoa! I'm bad like Barbie. I'm a doll. But I still want to party. I'm a 10, so I pull in a Ken. Like Jazzie, Stacie, Nicki."

"All the Barbies is pretty. **All the Barbies is bad.** It girls and we ain't playin' tag."

"Rad, but he spank me when I get bad. I'm an LA rodeo driver. I'm in New York, Madison Avenue. I'm a Barbie girl."

"The way Ken be killin' shit got me yellin' out like *Scream* house. Yellin' out, but we ain't sellin' out. We got money, but we ain't lendin' out. We got bars, but we ain't bailin' out. And that pink Ferrari we peelin' out."

So what's this about?

This is Barbie saying, "I'm bad."

Meaning, I'm hot. I'm bad. I'm awake. I'm alive. I play the game.

"I'm a 10 so I can pull in a Ken."

I play the game. He spanks me, but I'm playing. **I'm in charge.**

"Now we're yelling out," meaning sexually we're yelling, but we're not selling out. **We're playing the sexual game, but it's just part of our power.** It's part of my pink Ferrari. It's Bob Dylan.

"But really that pussy's so cold, we just chilling out. They'd be yelling, yelling, yelling out. It's Barbie, bitch, if you still in doubt. And I'm bad like the Barbie."

"I'm a doll, but I still want to party. I'm a 10, so I pull in a Ken. Barbie ain't nothing to play about. He wants to play in the play-house. The fuck they gonna' say now?"

In other words, what she's doing is saying we're in charge. We're the Barbie, bitch. We're the bad Barbie. We're the hot Barbie. **We're playing with Ken. We're moving Ken around.**

"Yeah, I know the trick, so I got him bricked. Yeah, I know the trick, so I got him bricked. And I'm bad like the Barbie. I'm a doll, but I still want to party."

It's kind of a play.

And then at the end it says,

"Okay, you can brush my hair, undress me everywhere, imagi-nation."

It plays with the old 1997 song.

But in this song, there's no "I love you."

There's a kind of rejection of the narrative of the first song, in which basically you have the gaze of male desire that defines Barbie.

Now Barbie has assumed her autonomy. She has assumed her power.

She's playing with her sexuality. Like Barbie says at the end of the movie, she says, "I'm here to see my gynecologist." It's the very last scene in *Barbie*. She's playing with her sexuality, but that sexuality is not for Ken. That sexuality is not for the love story. It's another expression of her power. That's the point.

She's playing in desire, but **she's not playing in desire because there's an intrinsic love or tenderness or fierceness** as the parts are seeking to come together in a larger whole. That's not what's happening.

Sexing and desire is an expression that *Barbie is bad. Barbie is the bitch. Barbie's hot.* Barbie's in her power. So it rebels against the first song.

It fits into the theme of feminine empowerment in *Barbie*, but there's no actual intimate communion with the masculine.

It is Barbie breaking through to a degraded level-two femininity, claiming her independence, without any capacity to invite and welcome Ken. There's no Eros.

It's a pseudo-erotic cynical claiming of desire as just part of my field, utterly divorced and dissociated from the sacred.

So that's the response.

That's exactly what *Barbie* is. That's what's defining culture.

CHAPTER 9

DESIRE, DEATH AND VALUE / IT'S ONLY LIFE AFTER ALL

In this chapter we analyze the *Barbie* movie, through the prism of another key song, "Closer to Fine" by the Indigo Girls. Even as modernity (and then postmodernity) implicitly rejected the reality of value, we—as a culture—still assumed that love is always going to be real. The point of *Barbie* is that it is not; *Barbie* is postmodernity on steroids at the very center of culture.

NO FIELD OF VALUE IN "CLOSER TO FINE"

"Closer to Fine" appears three times in the movie. It also appears in the trailer of the movie, meaning it's *the anthem* of the movie. Again, it's not that the makers of the movie fully understood what they were doing. That's not the point. Again, as we always say, this is culture speaking.

The song seems to be this very sweet song, **but the whole point of the song is that there's no intrinsic value, there is no Field of Value.** There's nothing that is, as the lyrics of the song say, *definitive.*

The first time this song appears is when Barbie is going to the real world. She is driving in her car and her singing of the song gets interrupted by Ken. What interrupts the song? Ken. **The truth of this song is interrupted by Ken.** Ken is standing for patriarchy. What's Ken going to be arguing for? **Value and love are real.**

The second time the song appears in the movie is when Barbie, Gloria, and her daughter Sasha are driving back to Barbie Land.

The third time we see Gloria and Sasha, mother and daughter, driving in the car. Initially we think that it's Sasha playing with Barbie dolls in the real world, but it's actually her mother Gloria. Sasha's dolls were put away and Gloria took the dolls out. It's Gloria who is having irrepressible thoughts of death, and thinking about cellulite, which is impacting Barbie in Barbie Land. It's this connection between Barbie and Gloria that begins the movie. As we've already mentioned, the only love story in the movie is between the mother and the daughter.

In this scene where they are singing "Closer to Fine" in the car, we see a little moment when Sasha looks over to her mother. There are six scenes in the movie showing the gradual falling in love of Sasha with her mom. So there *is* a great love story in the movie, but it's a biological love story between Sasha and Gloria. *That's* the real love story.

That's actually the structure of the movie.

How does the song "Closer to Fine" go?

> *I'm tryin' to tell you somethin' about my life,*
> *Maybe give me insight between black and white.*
> *But the best thing you've ever done for me,*
> *Is to help me take my life less seriously.*
>
> *'Cause it's only life after all, yeah,*
> ***It's only life after all.***

So, I am trying to discern, trying to understand my life. And—
The best thing you ever done for me,
*is help me to **take my life less seriously.***

Okay great, let's take our lives a little less seriously. Does that sound good? Sure it does. But what's the point here?

Less seriously here means with less gravitas.

Less seriously means *it doesn't matter.*

Why do you think this whole fucking thing matters so much? Relax, the thing doesn't matter at all. That's what the song is saying. Listen to it.

"It's only life after all."

This is one of the key themes of *Barbie.*

You cannot understand the world in terms of value if this life is all there is.

The theme shows up when Ruth Handler, who is the creator of Barbie (and thus a God figure) says to Barbie,

> "Being a human can be pretty uncomfortable. Humans make things up like patriarchy and Barbie just to deal with how uncomfortable it is. And then you die."

You want to become human? They just live and die. And they make shit up along the way because they're uncomfortable. So they make ideas up. And then you die. Why would you want to do that?

That is Barbie's creator speaking.

In the song "Closer to Fine," *Barbie* does a caricature of the definitive, a caricature of the Field of Value, and rejects it in toto. So what we have left is an isolated, separate self in a universe in which there is no love story, in which the closest we are to "fine" is to abandon any search for value at all and **just live your life until you die.**

Which brings us to the next point.

THE RELATIONSHIP TO DEATH

Let's talk about the relationship in the movie to death.

How does this movie think about death?

We've briefly mentioned the scene in the beginning of the movie, where Barbie is doing this all-girls dance night. In the middle of the dance, she suddenly asks, "Do you guys ever think about dying?" The music stops, followed by a long uncomfortable silence. Then Barbie corrects herself by saying, "I don't know why I just said that. I am just dying to dance!"

She is Stereotypical Barbie. She suddenly has this feeling that, *Oh my god! I'm thinking about death.* And we're not sure, and she's not sure herself, why is she thinking about death?

She gets up the next morning, and the song "Barbie" comes on,

> *When I wake up in my own pink world.*
> *I get out of bed and wave to my home girls.*
> *And they say, 'Hey, Barbie, why so stressed?'*
> *Could it be those irrepressible thoughts of death?*
> *And they say, 'Come on, we got important things!'*
> *It's pink, goes with everything.*
> *Beautiful from head to toe.*

So the song goes, "Okay, I'm Barbie, pink, head to toe." But where before the song went: "PINK: P, pretty, I, intelligent, N, never sad, K, cool," it now says:

> *P: Panic*
> *I: I'm scared*

N: Nauseous
K: Death.

So that's the song. That's the song. In this second version of the song that plays when Barbie is having irrepressible thoughts of death, it says, "P, Panic, I, I'm scared, N, Nauseous, K, Death."

It comes up in Barbie, the very next morning.

So Barbie wakes up the next morning and she has cellulite. Her legs are kind of not looking like she thinks legs should look like in public. She has thoughts of death and she's melancholic. She's kind of depressed, like *oh my god! What happened to me?* She has this sense of depression and death, and she has flat feet. Her feet are flat. All of this comes together and she's utterly devastated.

She's Stereotypical Barbie, but she has *irrepressible thoughts of death.* She tries to overcome it. She tries to say, *Oh, I'm not thinking about death anymore, I'm better, I was just dying to dance!*

But the **thoughts of death** come back the next morning.

It's the irrepressible thoughts of death that Gloria has in the real world, which then leak into Barbie. Now Barbie is thinking about death. She's thinking about death and cellulite. She doesn't know what to do with it.

The next day, her friends look at her and see that she has flat feet, and she is embarrassed. She's talking about death, cellulite, and flat feet, meaning she's talking about fragility and powerlessness, and death and mortality. She's embarrassed.

We're embarrassed by things that remind us of our mortality.

So, all of a sudden, you have this whole new play here. Death. And that's what sends Stereotypical Barbie to go to Weird Barbie.

She's forced to go talk to Weird Barbie to work it out.

She goes to Weird Barbie, who says, *You're in trouble. Because somebody must have been playing too hard with the doll in the real world, and there's been some interchange between you and that real world, between the Barbie archetypal world and the real world.*

Weird Barbie says, "You have to go to that real world and make it right."

So Barbie goes on that journey. **The archetype of *the experience of death*, goes on this journey to try and somehow make it right.** That's the story.

But she doesn't succeed in the journey. When she gets to the other world, a number of very beautiful things happen—but none of them add up. There's no plotline.

There's this intimation in the movie that never gets realized. Goddess has just dropped it in, but it's never realized, it's never closed.

But actually, death tells us something.

Death is important.

It's telling us something.

But the movie never gets there—it doesn't know what to do with death.

Barbie's basic assumption is:

- Thinking about death ruins the story. It gets in the way.
- Because we actually want to live in this illusory world **where we ignore the question of meaning.**
- Meaning is not real.
- Value is not real.
- Value is not real because you live *fucking* once, and then the whole *fucking* thing is over.
- Mother Teresa or Hitler—nothing actually matters.
- We are not going to say this overtly, but basically, there is no Field of Value.

- There cannot be a Field of Value because you cannot understand the world in terms of value if this life is all there is.

In his *Red Book*, Jung writes, "I cannot establish mental stability in a patient unless I can give them access to the realization that there's life beyond the boundaries of this life."

The religions hijacked that: *Oh, sure, there's immortality. We happen to know the way, and there is a cost. The cost is you do it our way. If you don't do it our way, you have no immortality—and it looks exactly like this.*

Wrong, wrong, wrong.

But what do we do in this massive, correct rebellion, in this evolutionary thrust forward, after we reject the caricatured versions of harps and heaven?

With our rebellion against religious versions of immortality, we actually rejected our innate knowing, as Harry Chapin sings in his song "Circle," *I have this funny feeling that I'll be back once again.*

It's why when you fall in love with someone, when you really fall madly in love, what do you say? I'm going to **love you** *forever.*

Now, *forever* doesn't mean everlasting time. It doesn't, by the way, necessarily mean that we'll ever meet again, in the way we met in this lifetime. **But it does mean that the essence actually continues, that there is a continuity of consciousness.**

You know, Bertrand Russell, the great atheist of the 20th century, says, *I don't know how to work out value theory.* He says, "I cannot see how to refute the arguments for the subjectivity of ethical values." Russell, a mathematician and philosopher, **gets caught in the assumption that value is not real** because it reigned in the day. He wasn't able to think his way out of that. But, he says, "I find myself incapable of believing that all that is wrong with wanton cruelty is that I don't like it." That's a direct quote from Russell.

"*IT'S ONLY LIFE AFTER ALL*": THERE CANNOT BE JUST ONE LIFETIME

In our body, we know that *fairness* is real. We all know fairness is real. We have cross-cultural information that one of the loudest cries of a child is: "It's not fair!" That's pre-culture. It's the beginning of language. When you feel fairness has been violated, there is this scream, this primal scream. There's an enormous amount of developmental literature about this—across time, across cultures.

Okay, so we know fairness is real. It means justice is real, in some fundamental sense; justice is a real category.

Of course, I get that there are perversions of justice, and that there is law, and that there are social constructions. **But the idea that it should be fair is a fundamental structure that lives in us.**

Yet there is no question that, for the majority of human beings, it's *not* fair in one lifetime. That's just true. The truth is, it's not fair for the majority of the world.

One lifetime does not create fairness.

- There is no equal distribution of talent.
- There is no equal distribution of wealth.
- There is no equal distribution of possibility.
- There is no equal distribution of joy.
- There is no equal distribution of sexuality.
- There is no equal distribution of beauty.

The list goes on and on and on.

So:

1. Fairness is real.
2. For the majority of human beings, fairness does not happen in one lifetime.

But if I know absolutely in my body that fairness is a real category—that Reality *demands* fairness, and I know that fairness has not worked out in one lifetime, then what else do I know?

3. I know there cannot be just one lifetime. So I know that there's a continuity of consciousness.

Now, I didn't resort to any of the evidence of reincarnation, of which there is an enormous amount. I didn't resort to the philosophical analysis of materialism and dualism. I left that off the table. I didn't go for any of the other kinds of empirical evidence that David Ray Griffin writes about, all of which are real.

I just talked about what lives inside of you. It's a big deal.

The movie *Barbie* says, *No. There is no continuity of consciousness.*

That's the postmodern assumption. It's literally a dogmatic assumption.

I talked to a very, very famous scientist, an excellent scientist. And he says: "I'm a stone-cold atheist."

I said, "Okay. Let me go to the evidence. I will walk you through one piece of evidence at a time. I will show you that based on every way that you evaluate evidence, there is no way to avoid the conclusion that there is a continuity of consciousness."

He said, "I'm not going through the evidence with you. I know what I know."

I've known this guy for years. He would *not* have a conversation with me.

That's dogma. It's complete dogma.

The movie adopts that same assumption that there is no continuity of consciousness.

God (in the form of Ruth Handler) says to Barbie, *Why would you want to become a human being? You live and you die. And they get uncomfortable, so they make up meaning. Don't do that, stay in Barbie Land.*

And yet—just like Arwen in *The Return of the King* who wants to become mortal—there is something in Barbie, who holds the best of humanity and has this yearning to become human in a way that Ruth doesn't quite understand.

This was all an explanation of the line in the song "Closer to Fine":

It's only life after all.

POSTMODERNITY ON STEROIDS

And then the chorus goes:

"Closer to Fine" Chorus

I went to the doctor, I went to the mountains.
I looked to the children, I drank from the fountains.
But there's more than one answer to these questions,
Pointing me in a crooked line.
And the less I seek my source for some definitive,
The closer I am to fine.
The closer I am to fine, yeah.

"There's more than one answer to these questions," meaning pluralism, meaning a rebellion against one answer. That's good. We *should* rebel against one answer.

But what she's actually saying is: "There's more than one answer to these questions, pointing me in a crooked line." This is *the line-quality*. Whenever something is true, it's written all over culture. It's pointing me in *a crooked line*—meaning lines are crooked. Answers are crooked.

Here is the next line.

"And the less I seek my source for some definitive
(The less I seek my source)
Closer I am to fine, yeah."

Definitive, meaning anything that's intrinsically so. Definitive means definitive. It's real. **In other words, *the less I seek my source in anything that's real.***

What the lyrics of the song are saying is: *I actually acknowledge that there are lots of answers. But the point is, none of them actually matter. You live once, it's all made up. We make them up because we're uncomfortable.*

This is the central meaning of the lyric of the song:

The love story is not real.

There's no Barbie and Ken.

Value is not real.

The Field of Value is not real.

There's no definitive answer. You live once, it's over. The whole thing's made up.

The best thing you've ever done for me is to help me take this life less seriously.

There's no gravitas in this life. Don't try and look for it. The more I get that, *the closer I am to fine.*

Now in case you think I missed this, just take a look at the last verse. This is what happens when you go look for some depth.

"Closer to Fine" Verse Three

I went to see the doctor of philosophy,
With a poster of Rasputin and a beard down to his knee.
He never did marry or see a B-grade movie.
He graded my performance, he said he could see through me.

And I spent four years prostrate to the higher mind.
Got my paper, and I was free.

You know who Rasputin was? Grigori Rasputin, a Russian mystic, was this controversial figure who's manipulative and controlling and destructive for the sake of power. So the doctor of philosophy has "a poster of Rasputin and a beard down to his knees," which is obviously not sexy. He never marries. He doesn't know anything about that stuff. "He never saw a B-grade movie." You wouldn't want to hang out with the dude. "He graded my performance." He is all *line.* In other words, it's mocking it.

"I spent four years prostrate to the higher mind. Got my paper, and I was free." Then I realized, no, no, no, these answers to these questions, it's all a crooked line. We read the Bible, that didn't work. Or we did the workout thing, that didn't work. We read up on revival, that didn't work. Oh,"there is more than one answer to these questions, pointing me to a crooked line. And the less I seek my source for some definitive in the real, the closer I am to fine."

You could still read this as kind of a sweet pluralism, there's more than one answer to these questions. It's a rebellion against fundamentalism. That's the good step. That's the positive step.

But then it says there's nothing definitive. Definitive doesn't exist. Meaning, there's no intrinsic value. There's nothing definitive. There's nothing that's an *ought.* There's nothing that's intrinsic in the structure of Cosmos.

And the more I realize that there's no source in any definitive, meaning it's all just perspectives, *the closer I am to fine.* Meaning, the more I try to attach to anything definitive, the more I collapse.

The movie is identifying intrinsic value or the definitive with its pathological form.

It's a modern movie saying: *Who has something definitive? Crazy people who make holy wars. Who has something definitive? Ethnocentric hijacking, which says that this is the right way.*

But that's not correct. That's a caricature of the definitive that defined the premodern part of the modern world.

But actually:

- There's a higher-level definitive.
- There's a Field of Value.
- There are First Principles and First Values.
- From those First Principles and First Values, we have a shared Story of Value, which is a context for our diversity.

None of this appears in *Barbie* at all.

This, my friends, is postmodernity on steroids at the center of a central movie, and at the center of culture. And no one even realizes that this is the text.

The reason there's no Barbie and Ken is because how *could* there be Barbie and Ken?

To say that there's Barbie and Ken would be to say:

- There is a value at the very center of Cosmos
- That value is Eros
- That Reality is lines and circles all the way down and all the way up
- That Reality is a love story

Someone said to me last night—it was a very beautiful and yet very sad thing: "Wow. In my generation, no one does sex, no one's interested. Yeah, there's some sex happening. But basically, the sense of Eros, the sense of sex, is not interesting. It's not happening."

And so Barbie and Ken don't have genitals, and certainly, their genitals don't point them to each other.

At the end of the movie, Barbie is going to go to the gynecologist but it doesn't have anything to do with Ken. She is claiming her sexuality independently of Ken. And "Barbie and Ken" could be, you know, "Barbie and Cindy," that's not the point.

Again, the point is: there's no love story at the center.

CHAPTER 10

ONLY A STORY BEYOND DEATH CAN STAND AGAINST EVIL

THE REALITY OF DEATH IN THE REAL WORLD MEANS LOVE MUST BE SOMETHING WE'VE MADE UP

In *CosmoErotic Humanism* we recognize two shocks of existence:

- The first shock of existence is the realization—at the dawn of human existence—that "the skull grins at the banquet." Life, before it continues, is first confronted by death. The first shock of existence is the death of the individual human being.
- The second shock of existence is the death of humanity, or in a second form, the death of *our* humanity—which we call existential risk.

The two shocks of existence are deeply related. The first shock of existence, the realization of the inevitability of **the death of the individual human is perceived as a challenge to the love story of existence itself.**

Indeed, in *Barbie*, the doll's creator Ruth—who is a type of Goddess figure—believes that all of Reality is a social construction. She creates the Barbie doll in order to create an imaginary world that is more beautiful and real then the socially constructed world. She basically says that all meaning is made up, and then people die and it's all over, that no meaning remains after death.

If death exists, if that's all there is, then how could love (or anything else) be real? (But if we realize, however, that if **love is real** then there must be continuity of consciousness.) This is the subtle, implicit theme of *Barbie*—almost certainly not intended by her writers. Rather, in a sense, this is culture itself speaking: She, the Goddess, is speaking through the voice of the contemporary cultural text of the movie.

The cultural text of *Barbie* proclaims that **because of the unavoidability of death, there is no love story in Cosmos.** Love is just not real.

This is implicit in the death scene, and is unpacked gradually throughout the movie.

The death scene, which is also a dance scene, represents the human realization of death—the first shock of existence—but in a postmodern context where any sense of the continuity of consciousness beyond death is denied.

The dance/death scene happens early in the film. As they are dancing, something happens. Barbie experiences and feels into her own personal death. In other words, she starts to ask, where is this all going?

At the end of the movie, when Barbie goes to the real world to become a human, and she meets her human creator Ruth, who says, "You go into the world, you have one life to live, and then you die." That's an accurate representation of the general assumption in culture.

So in the scene, as all the Barbies are dancing, praising the perfection of their lives, at one point, Barbie asks, "Do you guys ever think about dying." There's a record scratch, and everything stops and goes quiet, as everyone looks at her. "I don't know why I just said that," she whispers to herself. And then she declares to everyone: "I'm just dying to dance." The music starts up again and everyone loves it. Despite this hint, this brief realization, *Barbie* doesn't address death in any real way. The question just remains in the movie, without it really being engaged.

Barbie has to go to the real world, and she has to actually encounter death.

What is Barbie's big encounter with death? Her big encounter with death is in her conversation with Ruth Handler. Ruth is an older woman. She's closer to the place of death. She has this conversation with Barbie about what it means to become human. Ruth says to Barbie, "Humans make up meaning, and then they die."

Why does death matter here? Why is death important in this story? Why does death matter so much?

> *Death matters because if death is real, and death is an ultimate end to everything, then death, in some sense, undermines the love story.*

Existentialism did its absolute best to say there's a love story—even though we all die and even though they said there's no Field of Value and no plotline in Reality. In existentialism there's no story in Reality. There's no ontology of story. There's no plotline. There's no continuity of consciousness—but *somehow love is real.*

> *In other words, what the movie discloses is the incapacity to hold the love story without a broader Field of Value.*

That's the point.

When the movie talks about death, what's the movie saying?

The movie is saying: there is no love story.

If you die in the end, how can the love story be real?

So Barbie's thinking about death and her thoughts about death are a contribution to her realization that there's no Barbie and Ken. That "Barbie and Ken" is a kind of window dressing of pseudo-eros. That Barbie and Ken, are a kind of amplified, inflated, blown up, pseudo-eros. But there's no real Eros.

Real Eros must encompass death. Love must be as strong as death, says Solomon, in the *Song of Songs*.

But if death basically overrides love, meaning, if at the end of the story, everybody dies, and there's no continuity of consciousness, and there's no justice, and there's no sense of a larger field which goes beyond death, then there's something vapid and empty in the love story.

To restore the love story, the movie would have to restore some vision of the continuity of consciousness beyond death.

The movie can't do that because we've killed all the gods except for Aphrodite. The only thing that remains is the love story, and we think the love story is going to survive even though it's over when it's over. But if it's over when it's over, the love story somehow doesn't survive.

Because when you fall in love, what do you begin to say to someone?

"Oh my god, let's be together *forever.*"

Forever—that's what we call eternal love.

We can't love each other unless we know that there's an actual forever.

If you can't love that deeply, if it's over when it's over, it is too painful.

If it's over when it's over, I can't actually open to love all the way.

It's only the continuity of consciousness as a possibility that opens up the love story. The movie is not willing to open up the possibility of the continuity of consciousness, so therefore the movie has to shut down the possibility of there being a love story.

Death actually arouses love.

Death actually arouses the possibility of love.

Death allows for a love story, because you can't actually have a love story unless you know that it's part of the fabric of a larger continuity of consciousness.

If there's a love story, there has to be a quality of forever. Love stories have forever. That's their nature. They go on.

There's something about love that transcends death. Love stops the field and you can grasp eternity. Love is that which holds the eternity that resides in a moment.

It's why when we love, no matter what's going on, we can somehow hold it, because love is underneath time. That's its nature.

Love is underneath time.

It transcends time.

It lives in time and it transcends time.

It's not of time.

In the lineage of Solomon, when the Temple is destroyed, the Holy of Holies—which was the center of the Temple—becomes the Song of Songs.[27] The Song of Songs is this love song, which lives in the taverns, and it lives in

---

27 For a deeper understanding of The Song of Songs, the Temple of Jerusalem, and the Holy of Holies, see *A Return to Eros* (Gafni and Kincaid, 2017), *Mystery of Love* (Gafni, 2013), and *Love or Die* (Gafni, 2024)

the homes, and it lives in the beds. It transcends time and it transcends the laws of time. The *Song of Songs* is *Holy of Holies*. Meaning, we can actually transcend a particular moment of destruction.

The lineage doesn't get destroyed because it lives in the love song. And the love song is eternal by its nature.

But instead of speaking of eternal love, *Barbie* says, "No, no, no, it's over when it's over."

THE DESICCATED MOTHER SPEAKS: "HUMANS MAKE MEANING UP AND THEN THEY DIE"

So let's take a deeper look at the scene, which we've touched upon briefly, at the end of the movie, where Barbie and Ruth Handler meet.

It is an incredibly beautiful track and an incredibly sad scene. First, let's just talk about its beauty for a second. You have this meeting between Barbie and Ruth. It's a woman-on-woman meeting. It's the Mother, a beautiful mother.

Barbie wants to become human. Let's look at the conversation she has with Ruth:

> **Ruth Handler:** "You understand that humans only have one ending. Ideas live forever, humans not so much. You know that, right? Being a human can be pretty uncomfortable. Humans make things up like patriarchy and Barbie just to deal with how uncomfortable it is. And then you die."

> **Barbie:** "I want to be a part of the people that make meaning. Not the thing that's made. I want to do the imagining. I don't wanna be the idea. Does that make sense? Do you give me permission to become human?"

> **Ruth:** "You don't need my permission."

Barbie: "But you're the creator. You... Don't you control me?

Ruth: "I can't control you any more than I can control my own daughter. I named you after her, Barbara. And I always hoped for you like I hoped for her. We mothers stand still so our daughters can look back to see how far they've come."

Barbie: "So, being human's not something I need to... ask for or even want? I can just... It's something that I just discover I am?"

Apparently, that's the truth. **You just discover you're human and the sharp line between the creator and the human is obliterated.** There's a lot of beauty in that.

On the one hand, the scene's very beautiful. This scene is the moment that rebels against classical religion *correctly*, but then thinks that it's going to be enough just to evoke the fragrance of life's intrinsic meaning and that that will actually carry us forward into the future.

I fully understand why Rilke thought that, why Nietzsche on his best days thought that, and why the transcendentalists in some sense had some fragrance of that, and certainly the existentialists. Sartre is all about this. Camus is all about this.

This notion, **this appropriate rebellion against dogma in the sense that *there's nothing definitive*.** That's the text that we saw in the song "Closer to Fine" by the Indigo Girls—there's nothing *definitive*. Just lots of different answers to everything. There's no actual definitive intrinsic Field of Value. *But don't worry about that—just live your life as if it had meaning, even though it does not.*

Do you get the paradox? This is existentialism at its most poignant and beautiful and tragic best and worst.

So it's a very beautiful scene. Barbie wants to become human, but it's very different than the becoming human of Arwen in *The Return of the King*, who becomes human because she wants to be with Aragorn, the true King of Gondor. Because here, the king and the queen (the archetype of Barbie and Ken) are actually considered to be *real*.

When Tolkien is describing the world, he's saying *the king and the queen are real*. The kiss of the king and the queen creates worlds because it's aligned with the Field of Value. So that is why Arwen says I'm going to become human and give up my elfin immortality. She wants to be with Aragorn because Reality is a love story, and because love is an eternal value of Reality itself, so **to step into love is to step into eternity**.

That's precisely *not* what's happening in *Barbie*.

- *Barbie* is a world in which death ends life, in which after death, there is only nothingness. There is no Field of Value. Humans make it up, it's not real.
- Barbie wants to become human in **this kind of existential leap of meaning into the meaningless**—knowing it's all meaningless—but she's going to create meaning even though the meaning is meaningless.

Welcome to existentialism.

The movie's essentially holding that sense.

The scene then goes on to play the Billie Eilish's song, "What Was I Made For."

As the song "What Was I Made For" is played, we again see these scenes of mother and daughter, and mostly women, and mothers and daughters with children, laughing. So it's the same kind of love story. These scenes are obviously good. They're obviously beautiful. They're obviously tender. They're obviously poignant, and the point is, "*Fuck* meaning, it's self-evident. Even though we know that it's not true and then you die."

So we thought we could create a world based on this. **We thought we could rebel against the old religion and that it would be enough to have this**

kind of general intuitive field that we can deconstruct and live in it anyway.

That's what we wanted to do.

We wanted to kill all the gods except for Aphrodite.

APHRODITE CANNOT SURVIVE WITHOUT THE FIELD OF VALUE

We wanted to borrow, to take out a loan of value from the Field of Value, but a hidden loan, not telling anyone about it.

But postmodernity came and called in the loan and said,

- Actually, if there's no Field of Value, then Aphrodite is not real.
- And then death ends it all, and it's absurd.

So existentialism does these two things at the same time.

Existentialism says it's absurd.

There's quite a few existentialist writers who went on to commit suicide. Existentialism was very influenced by Gnosticism, where the act of the Gnostic is to commit suicide, to not participate in the world which is ultimately meaningless, because to participate in that world is to participate in a field of evil and compromise and corruption and degradation. And yet, existentialism is unimaginably beautiful, at the same time. Existentialism is an affirmation of beauty in a field of meaninglessness as we rebel against the old religions.

The poet Rilke is exactly this. He basically blows up the Field of Value. There is no value. There is no field of meaning. There is nothing after death. And yet, every line of Rilke's poem is dripping with meaning. Every line is just stunning and gorgeous. Rilke thought that would be enough, but he was wrong. It doesn't work.

We have to establish a post-dogmatic Field of Meaning, a post-dogmatic, post-ethnocentric, Field of Value. A Field of Value that's not just eternal, but it's also evolving. That's CosmoErotic Humanism.

That's what we have to do. We have to hold the mystery, and we have to avoid anything *definitive* in the sense of dogma, as the song, "Closer to Fine", points towards correctly.

We have to avoid anything definitive in terms of dogma, but embrace the definitive in terms of an intrinsic Field of Value in which we all live.

WHEN THERE IS NO FIELD OF VALUE, THERE IS NO DISTINCTION BETWEEN RIGHT AND WRONG

Let me say it differently.

Either there's an *ought* in Cosmos or there's not an *ought* in Cosmos.

We have to tell a story of the continuity of consciousness, which is a story beyond death, which means that there's an *ought* in the Cosmos. There's an *ought* in the Cosmos. **The *ought* in the Cosmos means you can draw a bright line between good and evil.**

But if there is no Field of Value, then **there is no ultimate distinction between right and wrong**. That distinction can't be drawn. It's an arbitrary distinction.

As Yuval Harari basically says, *there is no difference at all, in any ultimate sense, between massacring Muslims in the fourteenth century as a Christian young knight, and going to that same region of the world to work to heal refugees for Amnesty International. He says quite explicitly, those are both*

144

just made-up stories, and in a few hundred years, the story we tell now, the Amnesty International story, the positive Western value story, will also seem absurd to us. There is no ultimate distinction.

Someone very close to me is participating at the highest levels of the Israeli government in key moments of key decision making.

She was describing to me that Hamas is making recordings of children calling for help and putting them in alleys. They killed 10 guys that way. Dolls, all booby trapped. Hospitals, all booby trapped. Schools, all booby trapped. There's literally a *jihadi* state which is bent on the most depraved form of destruction.

Not to respond is moral insanity.

It's to have no ought in Cosmos.

It's why paradoxically, the *Barbie* movie is about the desiccation of the Field of Value.

There is no ought.

Nothing exists beyond death.

And that's exactly, essentially how Hamas understands the West: "You guys love life. We love death because we understand there's something beyond death."

So the Barbie movie sets up Hamas (or the old medieval ethnocentric, dogmatic, horrific versions of religion), as the people who hang on to life after death.

"We're just going to embrace the humanism of this life."

No.

We need actually to articulate something that embraces the best of humanism and the best of the realizations that there's a Field of Value which has a continuity of consciousness beyond this lifetime.

We need to have this moment of realization that we transcend death the same way that Hamas realizes that, but not in a way which is vicious and depraved, but in a way which is completely sacred.

But as long as we're holding on to that notion that it's over when you die, and Hamas is holding eternal reward in heaven, then they're going to win. Hands down.

You cannot defeat *jihad* with postmodern desiccated empty fields.

It's not going to happen.

You can only defeat evil with a stronger version of life, and a stronger version of life is the continuity of life.

It's the continuity of consciousness.

It's a Field of Value.

It's a Field of Value that has the continuity that there's a covenant between the generations.

"WHAT WAS I MADE FOR?"

When Ruth talks to Barbie, who wants to become human, she warns,

> "I can't in good conscience let you take this leap without you knowing what it means.
>
> Take my hands.
>
> Now close your eyes.
>
> Now feel."

Wind is blowing, pensive music is playing, "Feel this," and the Billie Eilish song plays:

> I used to float, now I just fall down.
> I used to know, but I'm not sure now.
> What was I made for?

In other words, I used to know, and religion used to have knowledge. But now, I'm not sure. I have no idea. *What was I made for?*

There is no Field of Value. There is no certainty. There's just this kind of strange, gaping uncertainty. This is what becoming human will mean.

> Taking a drive, I was an ideal.
> Looked so alive, turns out I'm not real.

That's now the feminine talking about itself. And it says,

> Just something you paid for.
> What was I made for?

> Because I don't even know how to feel.
> I want to try.
> I don't even know how to feel.
> Someday I might.

There's this aspiration. But I don't know how. **I don't know how to honor the Field of Desire.**

Look at the next stanza.

> When did it end?
> All the enjoyment.
> I'm sad again.

> Don't tell my boyfriend.
> It's not what he's made for.

> What was I made for?"

Meaning the Field of Desire between he and she, between Barbie and Ken has *ended*. So the same thing appears in the Billie Eilish song, "Don't tell my boyfriend," because this is supposed to be self-evidently good.

We killed all the gods except for Aphrodite, but it's empty and it's desiccated. I'm not even allowed to say it out loud.

This is Billie Eilish. She's that exact moment. That kind of confused, sweet, beautiful kid who's like, "What was I made for?" She doesn't know where to go. We think it's okay, cause we have Aphrodite, we still have the love story, but that's not true anymore either.

Eilish writes in the song,

> *Think I forgot how to be happy.*
> *Something I'm not, but something I can be.*
> *Something I wait for,*
> *something I'm made for,*
> *something I'm made for.*

There's **no dignity in the Field of Desire.**

These are the words to the song that Ruth Handler plays for Barbie as she wants to become human.

There's this yearning, this waiting. Because I don't know how to feel, but I want to try. **There's this yearning, there's this aspiration, but there's no *knowing*.**

- How do I get from *Waiting for Godot*,[28] who never arrives, to waiting for *messiah*?
- How do I get beyond kind of an empty *Waiting for Godot* to this yearning and this active waiting, this active participation in the evolution of love?

---

28 *Waiting for Godot,* play by Samuel Beckett.

So, the Billie Eilish song captures this desiccated Cosmos, captures this empty Universe, this broken Field of Value.

THE HOLY DANCE BETWEEN REVELATION AND MYSTERY

So in the movie, we get this sense that death ends the love story and that there's nothing beyond death. We get this sense of this tragic existential attempt to hold on to Aphrodite, even though we know she's not real, and we know there's no ultimate meaning, and we know that we die, and yet we still ask *what was I made for?*

There has to be a dance between revelation and mystery.

In the book on First Principles and First Values,[29] there's a list of 18 First Principles and First Values, and they're all formulated in equations. **One of the First Principles and First Values is the relation between revelation and mystery. That is a First Principle and First Value of Cosmos.** There's stuff that we know and there's stuff we don't know. There's holy mystery and there's revelation.

- **Mystery was solved, it seemed:** Right before the quantum revolution, there's a whole series of leading-edge scientists who are widely quoted, saying, "We basically solved it all. We've ended the mystery."
- Suddenly, quantum physics explodes, laughs, and says, "Quantum indeterminacy, you can't figure anything out. You can't track anything. You don't even know if it's a wave or a particle. You thought you knew the basic structure of Reality, you don't know a thing. Double-slit experiment, Copenhagen theory, **we have no clue what's going on with the mystery.**"

---

29 *First Principles and First Values: Forty-Two Propositions on CosmoErotic Humanism, the Meta-Crisis, and the World to Come* (David J. Temple, 2024)

- **Mystery was devalued:** Then there's the whole postmodern move that says, "All there is, is a mystery, but the mystery is dissociated from the Field of Value." When the mystery is an expression of the Field of Value, then I revel in the mystery. I'm in the rapture of the mystery. When the mystery is ruptured from the Field of Value then the mystery turns into, "What was I made for? *Fuck!*" And it's kind of a desiccated uncertainty.

But there's actually a kind of a *holy* uncertainty, which is the holy mystery. **That uncertainty dances with certainty.**

What am I certain about? I'm certain that it is valuable for us to do this evolutionary sensemaking on the movie *Barbie*. I'm sure this has great value and it makes *She* dance. I'm sure that it is valuable to stay in and kind of make it till the end. So this matters. This is a significant and intrinsically valuable and a holy and sacred thing to do.

There's an ought in Cosmos, there's an ought, something ought be done.

So the three great questions of CosmoErotic Humanism are:

- Where am I?
- Who am I?
- What ought be done?

There's an *ought* in Cosmos. **Without an ought in Cosmos, you can't make any distinctions.** You can't evaluate anything because there's no value. You can't evaluate without value.

There's revelation and mystery.

What Barbie says, which is basically what a desiccated postmodernity says, "There is no revelation. Revelation is all dogmatic." All revelation is characterized as dogmatic and ridiculous. All there is in *Barbie* is *what was I made for?*—without any certainty.

But that's just not true.

We live our lives based on a series of core certainties that we have direct access to in our bodies.

We know that it matters to love.
We know that fairness is a real structure of Cosmos.

It matters.

Children cross-culturally know "It's not fair!" as a problem. It lives even in the animal kingdom.

We know that Beauty is real.

We know that Goodness is real.

We know that there's something called Truth.
We *know* that.

There's an enormous amount that we know.

So that knowledge is real. It tells us something real about the Cosmos. It discloses value and its value is like air. It's like space. It's like time. There's space and time and value. They're inescapable.

We live within a Field of Value.

We have an Eye of Value.[30] There's an Eye of Value. We *see* value. Of course we do. We have to *codify* that, because **we live in a world that doesn't have a shared story, which is ripping itself apart in a meta-crisis.**

We can't create coherence or resonance without a shared Story of Value, so we have to codify value—but not dogmatically.

We have to say that there's a structure of value. We're in a Field of Value. Those values are *evolving*, but they're *real*, they're *definitive*.

---

30 CosmoErotic Humanism makes the distinction between the Eye of the Senses, the Eye of the Mind, and the Eye of the Consciousness (which is the Eye of the Heart, the Eye of Value, the Eye of Contemplation, and the Eye of Spirit). See David J. Temple, *First Principles and First Values* (2024), 237.

Barbie posits a false dichotomy between certainty and uncertainty. Barbie says there is no certainty—and the movie's uncertainty is not of the sacred form. It's not within the Field of Value. It says, *we just don't know anything, and we all die anyways, and meaning's made up.*

No, there's a dance between certainty and uncertainty. There's a dance.

When I was young, I wrote two books called *Safek (Uncertainty)* and *Vadai (Certainty),* which for a period of time before I left Israel made their ways in many of these *Shavuot* (Hebrew festival, Feast of Weeks). People would tell me students were reading them under the cover of their other books. One book was about certainty. The other book was about uncertainty. The point was that certainty is not, *"It is* true," but *"I am* true." *I am true* is: I'm irreducibly valuable. I'm irreducibly unique.

My essential "I" participates in the essential "I" of the Divine. *I am true.*

Meaning, *I am value. I'm irreducible value.* That's why I have personhood. That's why for example it's not okay to collect information about me and micro-target me and steal my attention.

Uncertainty itself, the Mystery, is a quality of Reality.

Mystery is a sacred quality of Reality. It's more than uncertainty. It's Mystery.

So, there's this dance between mystery and revelation. That itself is a First Principle and First Value of Cosmos. It's beautiful.

There's a unique Field of Desire in which I reincarnate

So to recapitulate *Barbie*:

- **Number one,** *Barbie* offers us essentially a desiccated world, in which there's only a separate self, **there's only a broken separate self.** *Barbie* does not articulate anything close to the new narrative of identity in CosmoErotic Humanism, the Evolutionary Unique Self.

- **Number two, there's no Field of Desire. Desire has no dignity. Desire has no divinity.** You have an empty world without a love story, without any dignity of desire, in which you have basically broken selves trying to make up meaning in the best way they can. There's enormous beauty in that—Sartre's beautiful attempt—but it doesn't work.

This doesn't work. The world collapses. What we need to do is exactly the opposite.

To the question *What was I made for?* we need to answer: I *know* what I was made for. I was made to give my unique gift, to contribute value. And contributing value is *real*.

Walt Whitman in his poem "Oh me! Oh life!" writes, "That the powerful play goes on, and *you may contribute a verse*." It appears in a very famous movie that I've thought of doing a close analysis of several times, but have never done, called *Dead Poets Society*.

Dead Poets Society is making the same move as Barbie—if you read all of the songs, and you read all of the poems, and you read the text of the movie. Robin Williams has the boys at the school look at the pictures of the previous classes, and he says something like, *What are they now? They're now all just fields, and all just grass, and all just ground, and they've all died. But* **what you can do before you die, you can contribute a verse.**

Walt Whitman himself was completely confused. Whitman is gorgeous. Body electric. But he's confused. He's confused, but not in a bad way. He's what his time needed to be. They're rebelling. Whitman embodies transcendentalism, rebelling against classical religion. Reaching for this kind of wider spaciousness, this wider humanism, and what they thought was, *Okay, you die, it's over.*

BARBIE, HAMAS, AND OPPENHEIMER

Whitman is okay with death his entire life until he gets close to death. Then Whitman goes nuts. At the very end of his life, he goes ballistic. As he comes close to death, he completely can't accept the notion that he's disappearing. And he was right.

In other words, he wrote so elegantly about death, but suddenly he's facing his own death and he says, *No!* But not because he was crazy, not because he was insane, but because he felt the utter goodness of value and understood that all the value disappears—which he knew was impossible—if it ends in that moment.

It's not just that *I contribute a verse,* because that's the existential affirmation of uniqueness in the face of oblivion, which doesn't have any real meaning.

No, my contributing a verse is Divinity uniquely incarnate as me being me, participating in the writing of the cosmic scroll, which exists way beyond my life. There's a continuity of my consciousness and my unique consciousness.

There's no way around that.

Buddhists often say, *No, there's just a field of awareness.* But they bring in reincarnation from behind the scenes. *There's just a field of awareness. However, you reincarnate.* Really? There's just a field of awareness, but you're reincarnating? Explain that to me. Of course, you can't explain that intellectually. I've looked at the scholarship of Buddhism over 30 years and no one has a good explanation for this. The notion of reincarnation in Buddhism is an embodied intuition that it's more than a bland field of awareness.

There's a unique field of desire in which I reincarnate.

Meaning, the story's not over. There's a plotline. There's a story. Reincarnation means there's a story. That's the exact point of reincarnation.

So they think they believe in only awareness and then they bring in reincarnation behind the scenes.

Nicely done. Incorrect, but it's actually correct.

In other words, the reincarnation people basically say, *We reincarnate. There's a storyline.*

Correct.

So when Whitman says *contribute a verse*, that verse is real. That's what we're here to do.

PRACTICE: CONSIDERATIONS ON QUESTIONS OF DEATH

What's my relationship to death?

Do I experience myself as being needed by all of Reality?

You have to be straight about it. No bullshit. No nonsense, no bypassing. Do I experience myself as being needed, not just by a couple of people around me, but by All-of-Reality?

Can I access an experience of being needed by All-of-Reality?

CHAPTER 11

OPPENHEIMER—THE SPLITTING OF THE ATOM AS A FAILED LOVE STORY

The two major movies that released at the same time in the summer of 2023, were *Barbie* and *Oppenheimer*. So to better understand the cultural context in which *Barbie* takes place, we will now take a look at *Oppenheimer*.

The movie *Oppenheimer* is about Robert Oppenheimer, who was the father of the atomic bomb, and who conceived the *Los Alamos project*. The project's mission was to design and build the first atomic bombs.

Both *Barbie* and *Oppenheimer* blew the box office away. In this chapter we will see that these two movies are deeply related, and they are related to the deeper issue, which is always Eros.

It is always *She*.

It is always the Field of Desire.

It is always the Goddess.

OPPENHEIMER—THE SPLITTING OF THE ATOM AS A FAILED LOVE STORY

MATHEMATICS IS THE *FUCK* OF COSMOS

So, what happens in the movie *Oppenheimer?* Oppenheimer has this enormous love affair with mathematics.

He has this key conversation with Nobel Prize winning physicist Niels Bohr, when he's in Germany. Bohr says to Oppenheimer: "The important thing in physics isn't *can you read the music,* it's *can you hear it.* Can you hear the music, Robert?" So what he basically says to him is, *Can you see the equations? Can you feel it?*

There is this moment, in the beginning of the movie, when Oppenheimer tries to poison his teacher, Blackett, by presenting him with a poisoned apple.

He wants to go and hear the genius Niels Bohr, and the teacher says, *You don't know how to do experimental work.* Blackett insisted that Oppenheimer dedicate more time to lab work, while Oppenheimer felt his talents were better suited for theoretical physics. He runs off to listen to Bohr, and he asks Bohr the one good question. Then he comes back realizing he had almost poisoned his teacher's apple and tries to prevent it. Bohr picks up the poisoned apple and he's about to eat it.

So first off, this is all about eating the apple. It's about the danger of eating the apple. **The apple is always the apple of the tree of knowledge of good and evil in the garden of Eden.** So, there's this moment of eating the apple and it's about the poisoned apple.

Just note, it is not that anything we're saying here was the intention of the writers of the movie, at all. **This is the Goddess speaking through the movie, and using the writers to speak.** We have no interest at all in the intention of the writers. This is the Goddess talking. It's like I said to Lana Wachowski, the night that we watched *V for Vendetta* in Chicago, I said, "The fact that you made the movie is irrelevant in this conversation. You have no more authority over this movie. Let's look at the text of the movie."

She totally agreed. That's why she made *V for Vendetta* and *The Matrix*. She's pretty awesome.

So, let's look at what the text is actually saying.

First we have this poisoned apple. Who's poisoning the apple? It's actually Oppenheimer. So, you see this **very complex relationship to knowing.**

Then, when Niels Bohr asks him, he says, can you *feel* the equations? **So mathematics is about *Fuck*.** That's what all math is: *Fuck*.

All math is making love.

Mathematics is *Fuck*, that's what the whole thing is. Meaning, you *feel* the math. The mathematics actually live inside of you. The equations live in you.

Just like the brilliant mathematician Ramanujan, a famous young prodigy who came to Cambridge in 1920 or so, was *intimate with every number in the Universe.* That's what professor Collingwood, a professor, who is the head of the department who brings Ramanujan from India, says to Hardy: **"Ramanujan is intimate with every number in the Universe."**

That's mathematics.

Numbers are the *Fuck of Cosmos*. Mathematics and music are paired with each other. It's why Pythagoras talks about music and mathematics.

To feel mathematics is to feel the coursing Fuck of Cosmos through the equations.

If you can do the equations technically but you can't feel *the currency of Eros,* then you're not in the game.

That's what Niels Bohr is asking Oppenheimer: "Can you hear the music, Robert?"

Oppenheimer says, "Yes, I can."

And then, we see this moment of like 40, 50 seconds of something like a *medicine journey*. You just see him kind of *journeying*. We see beautiful imagery of stars exploding, lovemaking, wild nature, water drops... You feel him in the currency of the Eros of Cosmos. He's on this beautiful journey. He feels the music of the equations. He *feels* the mathematics of Cosmos.

THE SPLITTING OF THE ATOM

Now, at a certain moment in 1938, physicists figured out how to split Uranium. They figured out how to split the atom.

In a Universe of Eros in which atoms want to join, the splitting of the atom is a different movement.

Wow! We're talking about *splitting the atom*.

What does that mean to actually create division in the fundamental atomic structure of Reality?

It means the capacity for *unimaginable destruction*. That's actually what's happening.

THE FIRST GODDESS FIGURE: JEAN TATLOCK

As we said in the beginning of this chapter, there is always a deeper issue, which is always Eros. It is always *She*. It is always the Goddess.

So, who is *the Goddess* in the *Oppenheimer* movie? Who is *She*, who is the Goddess?

There are two Goddess figures in the movie.

First, there **is a central figure who's the first Goddess in the *Oppenheimer* movie. The first Goddess is Jean Tatlock.** Jean Tatlock was a 29-year-old young psychology lecturer that Oppenheimer has an affair with, early in the movie.

We have to watch the movie knowing that she is the Goddess.

Jean Tatlock, a woman who was a communist in the 40s, was very close to Oppenheimer. He wanted to marry her, she didn't want to, so he gets married to another woman, but he remains close with Jean.

Even after he started the Atomic Energy Project at Los Alamos, she calls him and he goes to be with her for a night.

It is a very complex story, but it's very important. She's the Goddess—in her beauty, but she is also *the Dark Goddess.*

In every tradition, you have what's called *the Dark Goddess.*

- *Kali* in Kashmir Shaivism and Hinduism is both light and dark. She is complicated.
- The *Shekhinah* in Hebrew wisdom is both the *em nor'a*, the terrible Goddess, and the beautiful Goddess.
- She is *Lilith*. She is a Lilith Goddess. Lilith is this complex, deeply alive, deeply erotic, deeply intelligent, deeply sexual Goddess, and the man, Oppenheimer, cannot quite hold her.

Jean Tatlock gets Oppenheimer in an enormous amount of trouble. In the end, he loses his security clearance in 1949, because an attempt to take him down uses the Jean Tatlock story against him—her suicide, and his visit to her.

"I Am Death, Destroyer of Worlds"

Oppenheimer is a major womanizer. I don't mean that as a negative word. For some reason, we've made *womanizer* into a negative word, a negative form of womanizing, but what we mean here is that Oppenheimer *loves* women.

We weren't there, we don't know if these were beautiful relationships, or not—we have no idea. But we do know that women were a major part of his life. **Eros, *Fuck* was a major part of who he was as a being.** But he can't quite find his way. He gets completely caught up in two things:

- One, social justice, Spanish Civil War.
- And two, he meets Jean Tatlock at a Communist Party event at Berkeley, at the university. They have this kind of allurement.

There's this incredible moment. It's an incredible nude scene with Oppenheimer and Tatlock in the movie. It's actually a new way of doing a nude scene in a movie. It is actually done really elegantly and beautifully.

In this scene, she is the Goddess. This is the moment where he's the line, and she's the circle. She's the Goddess. She's Eros.

He is the line driving forward through mathematics to create these break-throughs in Reality.

At a certain point, once *the atom has been split,* Oppenheimer immediately realizes—and every physicist in the world is thinking the same thing:

We can make a bomb.

Because what follows from the splitting of the atom is a series of mathematics and physics that basically leads to a bomb. He's now realizing this is going to happen. He understands that this is his destiny.

Oppenheimer and Tatlock deeply love each other. They have this deep erotic, primal relationship. *She's the Goddess.*

So there's this moment, this unbelievable moment where they're making love. She stops. She gets up. She's looking at his library, and she takes out something from the *Bhagavad Gita,* which is the text "Now I am become death the destroyer of worlds."

She says to Oppenheimer, "Read this." He starts to kind of explain what it is. She says, "No, read it."

Then she kind of sits on top of him and takes him into her as he's reading it. It's an incredible scene.

The *line* enters the *circle.*

She's taking him inside, as he is reading and saying…

"I am become death, the destroyer of worlds."

That's it.

That's the Goddess.

What the Goddess is trying to do is to actually bring the line and circle together.

This scene gets completely lost in culture's review of the movie. No one picks up on it. This is actually not intended by the directors. This is *She* talking. This is *She* talking.

Just notice. Let's be real careful. Notice what happens.

They're in the middle of *Fuck.* She stops, she gets off of him. So, you get that this is *deliberate.* She stops. It's in the middle of the course and currency of Eros, *Fuck.* She stops. She then turns to the books. She's searching for something. *Why* does she do that? You can feel that this is *She.*

She says, what book is this? And again, this is the Goddess talking. The Goddess is moving through this. She opens up the *Bhagavad Gita.* Then you see the actual text in Sanskrit. You see the shot of it. And she brings it to him, *read it,* he starts to explain it, she says *no, no, read it.* He starts reading, *I am become death, destroyer of worlds,* and she puts him inside her, and she rides him.

She is both birthing Reality and she is demanding that the phallus be encircled by the yoni. That's the point. In other words, she's birthing this moment, and she's demanding that it is in *hieros gamos.* It has to come from *hieros gamos—the marriage of the sacred masculine with the sacred feminine, the line and the circle.*

It's an incredible, incredible scene.

That's the Goddess.

She has ways that *She* whispers.

This is how *She* talks.

The Goddess Commits Suicide

Now, let's follow it through. He wants to be with her. There's a scene where he walks in and brings her flowers—because you bring the Goddess flowers. But what does she do with them? She throws them away. But he brings them anyway.

He says to her, "When you call, I'm always going to come." It's a precise line. He says, "I promise, doesn't matter what's going on, when you call, I'll come." **That's a commitment to the Goddess.**

They don't actually come together as a couple. He gets married to another woman. It's 1943. He's running *Los Alamos*. **But when she calls, he comes.** That meeting becomes the subject of enormous controversy later. They meet in this hotel room. They make love.

She has a very unique form. She has this kind of very particular form. She doesn't have a kind of model's body. She has a much more interesting body. She has this full body, right? She has a very particular body. **She has this full Goddess body.** You can feel the Goddess, you can feel the nourishing in her body. She has this very full interesting body. Again, the movie directors were doing casting, but **actually Goddess was doing the casting here.**

It's a very particular kind of beauty that she has, which you can kind of feel in the curve of her breast and her belly, and how it moves, she is very particular.

So, it's not the standard of culture, it's the Goddess.

The next morning, after they made love, they're sitting, talking. This time he says to her, "I won't come anymore if you call."

And she says, "But you said you would."

So he breaks the *hieros gamos*.

He stops responding when she calls.

He breaks the *hieros gamos*.

He's telling the Goddess that he has to cut off from her, and then she commits suicide.

The Goddess commits suicide.

THE SECOND GODDESS FIGURE: OPPENHEIMER'S WIFE

Now, a second Goddess figure enters, which is Oppenheimer's wife, Kitty. His wife remains completely passive through the entire movie. We don't know much about her. She's this fascinating figure. She lost her first husband in the Spanish Civil War. They talk about it. Then, she was married again. Oppenheimer basically, very clearly, takes her from this second marriage. He's like, *whatever*. He was like, *the marriage is not a wall* theory. So, they have this moment and he essentially takes her, and he basically tells the husband to step out. So, it's this kind of very crazy, wild, audacious moment.

But then, they can't hold it. They have a son together, but they can't *hold* the baby. It's this broken Goddess moment. They can't hold the baby, they can't raise the baby, they can't hold each other.

She feels his line. But again, the Goddess doesn't have a place. That's what's happening.

The Goddess can't be the Goddess.

Kitty's body is different than Tatlock's body. Her body is more classical feminine beauty, it's a different form, but *she can't nurture*. She can't be the Goddess.

There is something about his line that is killing the Goddess.

That's actually what it is. It's like, *wow*! If you notice it, it's all right there. It's all like literally right in front of you, but it's invisible.

But then, there's this moment where *She* emerges.

The conceit of the movie is the 1944 *Atomic Energy Commission* hearings which are about whether or not to revoke Oppenheimer's security clearance. That's the issue. He's in the seat at the head of the table, and Kitty is sitting there by his side. Lewis Strauss, this kind of ugly masculine McCarthy kind of guy, is running the interview, and he's clearly out to destroy Oppenheimer.

There's a certain moment when Kitty, his wife, takes the stand with him and she just wipes Strauss out.

She just kills him.

That's the Goddess.

She steps in and she kills him. Oppenheimer can't. She does it. **The Goddess wields the sword.** That's the moment.

So, there are two moments where *line* and *circle* come together in the movie. Twice.

- First, the beautiful love making scene, where Tatlock makes Oppenheimer read: *I have become death, the destroyer of worlds.*

- Second, when his wife Kitty shows up in her full feminine. She knew the Jean Tatlock story and she had to hear it retold again. She's hurt and yet, she's the Goddess and she wields her sword and she just wipes Strauss out, she cuts his head off. She's the one person who cut the inquisitor's head off.

Line and circle. *Hieros gamos.*

Again, none of this is noticed by culture's reviews. Once we've pointed it out, it's almost self-evident. It's that clear. That's how *She* works in a movie. **That's how *She* works. There's the movie and then there's this way that She speaks.**

This is the Goddess talking.

THE RELATIONSHIP BETWEEN OPPENHEIMER AND BARBIE

We could say a thousand other things on *Oppenheimer,* but this is all we need.

We're reading movies as sacred texts of culture. Again, the movies *Barbie* and *Oppenheimer* were released at the same time, in the summer of 2023.

Now, what is the relationship between *Oppenheimer* and *Barbie*?

- Both movies are about the dance between the line and the circle.
- Both movies are about breaking *hieros gamos.*
- **Both movies are about a failed love story.**

As we began this chapter, **in a Universe of Eros in which atoms want to join, the splitting of the atom is a *different* movement.** We're talking about *splitting the atom*. What does it mean to actually create division in the fundamental atomic structure of Reality? It means **the capacity for *unimaginable destruction.***

That's actually what's happening.

The splitting of the atom is a different move than the allurement of Eros.

It is that which generated the possibility for Oppenheimer, the father of the atom bomb, *I am death, the destroyer of all worlds,* to create the atom bomb.

Now let's return to Barbie and Ken.

Remember the song we talked about, "I'm Just Ken," where Ken is trying to figure out who he is? Barbie told him, *you're just Ken!* But that's actually not true. It's always Barbie and Ken.

In other words, **protons, neutrons, and electrons form an atom.** Atoms come together to form a molecule, molecules form a macromolecule. The molecule is not just a molecule. Macromolecules form cells. Cells form an organism, organisms form a body.

In other words, galaxies come together in particular relationships. **It's actually *Barbie and Ken,* all the way down and all the way up the evolutionary chain.** This is true at every level: at the subatomic level of three quarks that live together—without the three quarks, there's nothing, they disappear.

So the point is that it's actually *always* Barbie and Ken.

So what is actually happening in *Barbie*?

They're actually trying to split the atom.

They're literally splitting the atom.

In other words, they're splitting Barbie and Ken.

It's the same movement.

The atom is now being split.

The atom is Barbie and Ken.

That's the atom.

Culture says that it's a feminine empowerment movie. Or the best of culture says that it's a feminine empowerment movie that bashes men. Do you get how uninteresting that is?

No, no, no… culture is actually doing something far more insidious:

They're splitting the atom.

That is why, when you finish watching the movie, even though you don't understand it, you have a weird feeling in your body.

You're like, *ew, what was that?*

It's disturbing and you're not sure quite why, right?

It's because the movie is about affirming that the atom split.

The bomb has dropped.

There is no Barbie and Ken.

I have become death, destroyer of all worlds.

It's like… *wow.*

CHAPTER 12

THE FAILED LOVE STORY AT THE ROOT OF ALL EVIL: A CONVERSATION WITH DR. MARC GAFNI AND AUBREY MARCUS

Editor's note: This next chapter will have a slightly different style as it is a dialogue with Dr. Marc Gafni and Aubrey Marcus, on his podcast. As we are reading movies as sacred texts of culture, we need to be aware of the cultural context in which the movies are released. Therefore, in the following chapters we will dive deeper into the atrocities that happened in Israel on October 7, 2023, and see how the failed love story, as expressed in both Barbie and Oppenheimer, is at the root of all evil.

AUBREY MARCUS: INTRODUCTION

We are back at an insanely challenging and difficult and strange time in the world. One of the things that we've been talking about is that **so much**

of what we're experiencing is a failed love story. So much of the evil that exists in the world is because we've lost the plot of the Universe and our participation in the Universe, something you (Marc) call the CosmoErotic Universe. We've lost the plot of the love story and we've forgotten that we're the main characters in this love story. And when we forget the plot, we go off plot.

DR. MARC GAFNI: EVIL EQUALS FAILED LOVE STORIES: FAILED LOVE STORIES CREATE EVIL

You just summarized it beautifully, the very, very core of CosmoErotic Humanism. You and I have been in deep conversation about this the last couple of years, but particularly the last several months, as events in the world have exploded in so many ways. What I've been trying to point towards and what we've been talking about so deeply is, as you said, we have to get beneath the headlines into a place where we can actually make sense, where we can actually do sensemaking. We can engage in *the sensuality of sensemaking*, and really understand what's happening.

Now let's take the next step. We are reclaiming The Universe: A Love Story. It's an Intimate Universe.

At the very core of it is this equation:

Evil equals failed love stories. Failed love stories create evil.

Now that only makes sense if we understand that:

- Reality is not empty, Reality is full.
- Reality has inherent Eros and *telos* (direction).
- Reality is not merely a fact, Reality is a story.

This is so deep, because what we're doing is creating the ground of a new world religion *as a context for our diversity,* the ground of a new way of being in the world, the ground of what we might call the move from *Homo sapiens* to *Homo amor—the new human and the new humanity.* Each of us listening in our own lives actually can participate in that which actually makes life alive and wild and beautiful.

Let's begin to follow the thread and then we can deepen. What we've begun to understand is that:

- Reality is not really a fact, Reality is a story.
- Reality has a plotline.
- Reality actually has inherent in its structure a narrative arc.
- Reality is going somewhere.
- The plotline of Reality is the evolution of love.

It's just so stunning.

We don't mean this in any kind of retro-fundamentalist way, nor in a kind of tinsel, superficial kind of New Age way, but as **the deepest structure of the interior and exterior sciences.**

- Reality is not merely a fact, Reality is a story.
- Reality is not an ordinary story, Reality is a love story.
- Reality is not an ordinary love story, Reality is an Evolutionary Love Story, an Outrageous Love Story.

And then finally, and this is where it begins to become literally the single most real thing a human being could hear, which is that:

- My story, my personal story has a plotline.
- My personal story is also a love story and that love story is not separate from The Universe: A Love Story. It's not separate from the cosmic love story.
- My personal love story is a chapter and verse in The Universe: A Love Story.

All of this is just words until we learn it through the stories of our lives. Once I understand and truly grasp that these are not just words, but the ontological, the true, the real—it's more real than real, it's real, it's Reality. Once we get that, we realize: *Oh, if that's true, if it's a CosmoErotic Universe, an Intimate Universe, if it's The Universe: A Love Story, then living in denial of my own story's plotline leads to pathology, breakdown, and ultimately acting out.*

To go insane is to deny my identity, to deny my place and my nature—*I'm not in a love story.* If I'm not in a love story, then that's not just a psychological problem, that's not a mystical dilemma; but it's actually a violation of my core identity. So, let's take a couple of steps. First, we need to show that this is true. How do we know it's true? Why is it true?

BARBIE, OPPENHEIMER, AND HAMAS ARE AT THEIR CORE FAILED LOVE STORIES

On October 7th, there's this brutal, horrific attack, probably the worst atrocity against women in the last 80 years, with many men killed or kidnapped as well. But there was especially this kind of systemic abuse and rape and torture and dismemberment of women of all ages in front of each other—a horrific atrocity as Hamas enters Israel.

As that's happening, *Barbie* and *Oppenheimer* are playing in the theaters. It's an Intimate Universe.

These events seem to have nothing to do with each other at all, but actually *Barbie, Oppenheimer,* and Hamas are inexplicable unless you understand them. This is all absent both from the reviews of *Barbie,* the reviews of *Oppenheimer,* and from the news feeds of Hamas.

Barbie, Oppenheimer, and Hamas are at their core failed love stories.

That approach changes everything.

A failed love story creates evil.

There's actually a battle between good and evil. The battle between good and evil is the battle between love and un-love. It's the same battle.

But we need to understand what that means or we'll lose the battle.

172

SO WHAT DOES "THE UNIVERSE: A LOVE STORY" MEAN?

What does it mean that *Barbie* is a failed love story?

How would that create evil?

Barbie is telling the story of what you (Aubrey) like to call empire, the technocratic, techno-totalitarian move for control and for kind of undermining our essential humanity, which in the end leads towards evil in a very, very deep and profound and horrific way.

The story of Hamas is a story that has nothing to do with Israel, by the way. Israel's not part of this. It's a *jihad* story.

Jihad means *the struggle*. Most people struggle with faith, with its demands. But the way it's interpreted now in some parts of the Islamic world is that the struggle between good and evil is the struggle between a certain brand of militant extreme faith—which is essentially a culture of death against life itself—and the rest of the world.

It is life and anti-life.

Jihad is interpreted this way in Iraq and Syria with ISIS or the Islamic State, without Israel. It's happening in Yemen with the Houthis, and elsewhere. **So Israel's not actually the issue.** Let's take that off the table. That's a different and important conversation, which we've had at a different time.

But actually:

Hamas, at its core, is actually a failed love story. It's a failed story of desire.

So that's a beginning, my friend. We just literally shifted the world on its axis. It's a huge claim, but we're grounding it in all of the deepest interior and exterior sciences.

To begin to bring this new Story of Value to the world, which is actually this love story as an ontological Reality, is the only way to respond to suffering, to pain of the most horrific kind, and to the meta-crisis in general. **At its core, the meta-crisis is a failed love story.**

It's only the restoration of the CosmoErotic Universe, the Intimate Universe, that can actually lead us, take us home, personally and collectively.

AUBREY: WHAT WE MEAN BY WORLD RELIGION

Yeah. So let me gather a few threads and we're going to dive right into this.

First of all, you dropped the concept of *world religion* and I think it's just worth mentioning what we mean when we say that.

It's about understanding the Universe, and understanding the nature of Cosmos itself. And **whenever we, in CosmoErotic Humanism, say world religion, it's as a context for our own diversity**. You (Marc) lead a weekly teaching called One Mountain, Many Paths. There's many, many ways to understand the nature of the Divine and many different practices and many different tracks that you can take, which are all uniquely gorgeous in the way that they've been transmitted through the lineages. Of course, there's the unique challenges that have come with big capital-R religion as they've taken these divine sparks and then used them through the forces of empire to wield power and control—all of that. **But really what we're doing is articulating universal truths that allow for a context of diversity of how you worship, the names you use, and so forth.**

So I just wanted to drop in and share this with people who might've been thinking, "Oh, shit! World religion, what are they talking about?" No, no, no. **It means keep your faith, but let's all work together.** Instead of fighting over which God is which, which God is the awesome God, and which God you worship means that you need to be destroyed. We need to move well beyond that, so we can become one planetary civilization and system—not in the empire way, which is total control and a hierarchical pyramid with one person or one governmental agency at the top controlling everyone through force. Instead, we need a context for diversity, where all the different tribes, cultures, and nations are represented in their own beauty and allowed to flourish in their own unique way. So I wanted to pick up that thread.

MARC: A NEW WORLD RELIGION IS A NEW STORY OF VALUE AS A CONTEXT FOR OUR DIVERSITY

That's a big one. So let's drop into that for a second. It's really important. I say to our gang at the Center for World Philosophy and Religion, which you (Aubrey) are the Board Chair of, we have a kind of operative, sacred instruction, which is we never say the words "world religion " without ending, as you did, with "world religion *as a context for our diversity.*" For the very reasons that you just laid out so beautifully. It's **world religion always as a context for our diversity**, to avoid the sense of a totalizing homogeneity.

But when you think about the next step, **what is religion?** Religion is to *re-ligare. Ligare* is a ligament, but it's the connective tissue. It's the tissue of Eros. So to *re-ligare* is to reconnect. It means nothing is outside of the love story. **So all that *world religion* really means is that nothing is outside the circle and no one is outside the circle.** It's actually one love, and it's one heart, and it's one breath.

In this moment, my brother, we deeply understand the challenges of the meta-crisis facing our global world, and each of us participating in this conversation today has a sense of the whole, of the world, in a way that no previous generation ever did.

If you're listening in the United States, for example, a plane can fly into Manhattan and take down two towers—an attempt to cut off the balls of the West, if you will—and global is now local. Someone just went to work in the morning, and all of a sudden, a failed love story from some other part of the world came in and destroyed 3400 or 3500 people in a matter of seconds. So, there is no longer a sense of *local*.

We're actually *omni-considerate*, Buckminster Fuller's word, **for the sake of the whole.** That's *Homo amor, the fulfilment of Homo sapiens.* I feel the whole.

At that point, world religion becomes like breathing.

In other words, when we have local problems, you can have local religion, local *re-ligare*. Of course, that makes sense.

Now, by definition, if we don't have a globally shared Story of Value, then we have no intimacy, we have no shared love story, and then we have a *global intimacy disorder.*

And Aubrey, you and I are so deeply involved in so many different tracks and we are looking at how do we actually make this *da Vinci move.* Da Vinci—who, like us, also lived in a time between worlds and a time between stories—tried in the Renaissance to tell a new story, knowing that only this could challenge the Black Death, plague, pandemic, and societal breakdown.

So that's what we need to do today. We need to tell this new Story of Value. It has to be a world religion, and we have to not be afraid to say that, but it's always as a context for our diversity.

So the image is a Unique Self Symphony in which every religion is a unique instrument in the symphony, but all of them are playing the same music.

Music is Eros.

Music is love.

Music is the one love and one Eros that animates Cosmos.

After your next bracket, Aubrey, which I'm looking forward to, I want to talk about what we actually mean, so that friends don't think that we're just *declaring* this. This is not a fantasy. This is not a New Age declaration.

We are going to root this notion of The Universe: A Love Story before we go to *Barbie* and Hamas. So we get that this is real, this is not a fantasy. This is literally the most real Reality that exists, and not knowing this—**not knowing that the Universe is a love story and that I participate in that love story—is actually to be insane.** It's why so much of Western psychology doesn't work—because we're operating without knowing basic answers to the basic questions of our identity, the basic questions of *who we are*, and *where we are*, and *what ought be done.* We're trying to do this kind of papered-over psychology, which simply breaks down, it doesn't work.

So if I don't know that I'm in the Field of Eros, I'm in the field of *She*, I'm in the field of a love story—quite literally, the love story that lives uniquely in me—if I don't know that, then I can't actually function in the world. To go deep into that understanding is the most transformational knowing I can possibly have.

So that was just on world religion, which is critical.

AUBREY: WHAT IF YOUR LIFE HASN'T BEEN A LOVE STORY

Yeah, absolutely. I'm glad you opened that up and finished that thought. For sure.

Now, what I want to voice is just somebody who might be saying, "Well, fuck you guys, because my life hasn't been a love story. My life has been hard." That's also true that there are certain people who've had a really tough go at this. You can look at this in any culture. You could look for example at someone who's growing up in Palestine, and they're not jihadists, they're not supporting Hamas, but Hamas has taken control and limited their availability.

I mean, we saw this with Mahsa Amini in Iran. She's living in *a failed love story* where she's not able to live her own love story because the failure of somebody else's love story is then impacting her love story, and all of the tragedy of so many people who've died in the collateral damage in the conflict in Israel as well as the direct casualties. All of this is sometimes the failure of somebody else's love story, which prevents you from living your own *fucking* love story, which is why, again, **we have to universally affect the love story of the Cosmos, so everybody has a chance.**

MARC: THERE'S A SPARK OF THE SACRED IN EVERY BROKEN VESSEL

So what you're beautifully saying, Aubrey, is that we're no longer in a world where we can actually withdraw in our own world. The illusion that you could withdraw into your own world and live your private love story has been exploded by this moment in history.

So therefore, we have to move *from Homo sapiens to Homo amor.*

Homo amor is this new human who is omni-considerate for the sake of the whole, who knows that the Universe is a love story, and that it has to be one story.

There has to be a shared Story of Value as a context for diversity.

But let's go back to the "fuck you" for a second because it's so important.

There's no one whose story is not a love story. So even when my story fails, my story is a love story.

As you (Aubrey) and I have been talking about, I get a text thread every day with texts from Gaza, which is about people who have been killed in Gaza in the bombings. Innocent civilians whom Hamas has trapped and were not allowed to leave. As Douglas Murray pointed out, *if there's a colonizer in Gaza, it's Hamas.* That's quite clear, it has kind of been quite evident and tragic. So I get a thread of people who are killed in Gaza and then I get another thread of 18, 20, 21-year-old soldiers killed. The thread I have this morning was actually the worst day of the war. There were ten boys killed, from the time I went to sleep to the time I woke up. At least four of them, I knew, directly or indirectly, either their families or people connected to their families, or I have come across them. I mean, on all sides these were the most beautiful people in the world.

The reason murder is a tragedy, and the reason innocent civilians killed in a war is a tragedy, and the reason atrocities are atrocities, is because they're violating something.

In other words, evil is a failure of intimacy.

Evil is the opposite of life.

There's life and anti-life.

Evil is "live" spelled backwards, if you will, in its structure.

Evil in Aramaic is *sitra achra*, meaning, *the other side*. The other side is when I turn my back to you. We're no longer face-to-face; we're no longer in a love story.

The only reason that I'm suffering is because I understand that my life *should* be a love story.

The only reason evil is considered evil is because if the world were empty, as our colleague Sam Harris suggests, representing the traditions of reductive materialism, then evil wouldn't matter.

If the world is empty, if it's over when it's over, if death is the end of the story—which is one of the major themes, for example, in the *Barbie* movie—and all meaning is simply made-up, then what would be the tragedy of a life without love?

If meaning is simply made-up, then life is just the short little blip you have, and love is just a social construction—we made it up anyways. It's just something that makes you feel a little more comfortable in the few years that you're here and then *game over.*

That's the assumption built into both:

- **The fundamentalisms of postmodernity,** which generate *Barbie,* and which generate a kind of techno-totalitarianism in the making, which generate arms merchants, which generate a military-industrial complex, which generate a medical-industrial complex. The assumption is love is not real. Love is a complete social construction,

- **And Hamas dogmatism or *jihadi* dogmatism and fundamentalism,** which says that actually this world is *not* a place of ErosValue. Which says that this world is just a hallway leading to the 72 virgins in heaven. **In this world, desire is to be rejected, desire is degraded**. If I feel desire, that's an expression of a violation. So that's an example of a degraded love story, which itself leads to evil.

So it is only evil, it is only suffering, because we actually know in our bodies that it's *supposed* to be a love story.

That's why, brother, there's music all over the world, and throughout history, all music has universally been love songs.

It's not because someone dogmatically imposed it. **It's the voice of *She.*** It's the voice of the Goddess, the voice of the *Shekhinah,* the voice of *Shiva* and *Shakti,* the voice of Earth's Sky, of Yin and Yang coming together and saying, "Oh my god, I'm a love story, and so the songs that I'm going to sing, the music of Reality, will be love songs."

It's been that way forever. We sing love songs, whether it's a country restaurant with a truck driver or whether it's a Chinese version or whether it's an Indonesian version or an African version or something from New Zealand.

It's all love songs, because Reality is the mathematics of intimacy. When you violate the values of that equation, you create evil.

So just to take a moment to feel this together, brother, before you take us to the next step. We haven't seen any public sensemaking from legacy institutions—whether left or right, anywhere in the world—that truly attempts to understand what's happening. We haven't seen one place that actually talks about how there's a failed love story,

We need to understand this in the context of the battle between good and evil, because if I understand Hamas is a failed love story, then it changes how I approach the battle between good and evil. Understanding that no one is excluded from the love story means that even as I battle Hamas, and even as I may have to kill people who committed the worst atrocities of the last seventy years, I still don't place them outside of the love story.

It's different than for example a Zoroastrian position, which is *there's good and evil, and they're completely split.* That's one way to do the battle between good and evil.

But when I understand that the entire Universe is a love story, where nothing is excluded, then it's a love story that goes beyond this lifetime. There's a continuity of consciousness where even as I close my eyes in death, I open my eyes into a new Reality. **Then I realize that those people living in a tragic, failed love story still hold a spark of the sacred,** a spark of love. Even when we have no choice—because the world is being held hostage—but to protect this and future generations from harm, I still realize there's a spark of the sacred, there's a spark of love in every fallen love story, which changes the way we relate.

Let's just look for a second at Germany and Japan. Germany and Japan were the two centers of fascism and the worst forms of Nazism—evil.

When we talk about the world as a love story, it's actually shocking to realize that Germany today is a thriving democracy, and Japan is in multiple ways a thriving democracy, and they both had fierce failed love stories at the center of their culture. Japanese imperial emperor culture was a failed love story, an ethnocentric limited story in which love was limited and distorted. Germany was obviously a failed love story, Hitler was a failed love story—the love of the Aryan race in the most distorted and vicious form.

Both of those cultures in some deep way have evolved.

There's an evolution of love.

If we would just exclude them, we would just have to wipe them out forever.

But actually—

There's a way to actually be in fierce, full battle between good and evil and yet infinitely tender with this covenant between the generations, in which no one is outside of the story and there's a spark of the sacred in every broken vessel.

Wow! The Garden of Eden is not paradise, it's paradox.

AUBREY: HOW ARE WE GOING TO WEAVE BARBIE INTO THIS CONVERSATION?

Yeah. Wow! So then we planted a seed and some people are thinking, "*Barbie*? What the fuck does this have to do with Nazism, fascism, *jihadism*, all of these other things? Come on, Marc! What are you talking about? Let's get real here. This is a popcorn and bubblegum movie about a Mattel doll and it doesn't matter. And why don't we talk about some real shit?"

But you actually had a deeper reading of this as really a sacred text of culture. As you say so eloquently and so accurately, all of these movies are pointing to sentiments that are living in the fabric of culture itself.

You spotted some things in this film, which I never would have watched unless you made me watch it. So also, thank you and *Fuck you* for making me watch *Barbie*! But nonetheless, in watching it and then talking to you, I started to understand what you mean.

But there's going to be a lot of people listening who are going like, "How are they going to weave *Barbie* into this conversation?"

MARC: ONLY A DEEPENING OF THE LOVE STORY RESPONDS TO EVIL

Oh my god. Oh my god. So let's talk about *Barbie*. We have this like radical love commitment that everyone reading this will get very clearly for themselves why the Universe is a love story and an understanding of the relationship between Hamas and *Barbie* and how it affects each of our personal love stories.

So let's start with *Barbie*:

Barbie is a failed love story.

Hamas is a failed love story.

Jihad is a failed love story.

Barbie and Hamas are two forms of fundamentalism.

A failed love story equals evil.

So therefore, the battle between good and evil needs to be about deepening a love story.

Only the deepening of the love story responds to evil.

You can't do the battle of good and evil if you bypass the love story.

THE FAILED LOVE STORY IN BARBIE: RECAPITULATION OF SIX CORE SCENES

Editor's note: this section briefly recapitulates core scenes which are more deeply described in previous chapters.

So let's look at *Barbie*. It looks like this very innocent movie. It has a big piece of feminine empowerment, which is beautiful. It has this major de-monization of the masculine. There's not one positive masculine figure, ex-cept for the minor character of Allan, who only speaks twice in the movie. There's no positive masculine figures, but we're not going talk about either of these things. Let's talk about the very core of the movie.

As we've said many times before, *a movie is a text of culture.*

So when we're talking about *Barbie*, we're not talking about what the script writers Noah and Greta were thinking when they were hanging out in their apartment in New York as they wrote the movie. That is not our issue.

What we're concerned with, or what we're paying attention to, is how is God/Goddess speaking through the movie? How does Eros, how does The Universe: A Love Story, how does Spirit speak through a movie? How does *She* speak through the movie?

So let's just take a look at *She*. So let's just take a quick look at a couple of scenes in Barbie.

Scene 1: *"Girls' Night Every Night"*

If you remember, in the beginning of *Barbie*, there's a dance, a dance mo-ment. At the end of the dance, Ken wants to stay over and says, "Hey, I thought I might stay over tonight." And she says something like, "Why? Why would you stay over? Why would you even do that?" He said, "Well, we're girlfriend-boyfriend." And she says, "Well, what would we do?" And Ken is not quite sure. And she says, "No, you're just a friend and this is *my* dream house."

It's Barbie's dream house, and it's girls' night, and it's **"girls' night every night, forever."**

Ken's like, "It's girls' night every night like forever?" And she says, "Yeah, every night is girls' night." And she says, "Good night."

And then she walks inside and he kind of says half to himself, he says, "I love you too."

The point is, there's no one to say *I love you* to.

This is not Barbie, a particular person, projecting a particular thing. **Barbie is a doll. She's an archetype. She's a structure of consciousness.** This is "Barbie and Ken." Barbie says to Ken, it's "Girl's night, this night, every night, *forever*," meaning: there is no love story. It doesn't exist.

That's just one moment in the movie, but the theme of there not being a love story moves through the whole movie. It's a key theme.

Scene 2: *"I Don't Love Ken"*

There's a moment later in the movie when Sasha, the daughter of Gloria says, "Well, what about Barbie?" And Will Ferrell, the bumbling, masculine, patriarchal president of Mattel, says, "Oh, that's not a problem. Barbie loves Ken." And everyone says, "Ah, Barbie loves Ken."

And Barbie says, "No, I don't love Ken. Barbie does not love Ken."

But she's not saying, when you read the scene, *this* Barbie doesn't love *this* Ken. She's saying, **there is no Barbie and Ken.**

The notion that there would be a Barbie and Ken that is a structure of Reality is silly. **There is no love story.**

This is so deep, my friends. We thought that we could kill all the Gods and keep Aphrodite.

185

We thought we could kill the Field of Value and we'd keep one value, Eros, love. It doesn't work.

Along comes Barbie, and Barbie says, "There is no Barbie and Ken." It actually doesn't exist.

Love is only real, Eros is only real if it's in a Field of Value. It's part of The Universe: A Love Story, it's part of the structure of the Universe.

Scene 3: "I Thought This Would Be Our House"

So here's a third scene. We will see that this is not a contrived thing, if we actually read the movie carefully. Again it is not what Noah and Greta *intended*, but this is **Goddess, *She, Shekhinah,* speaking, and crying through the movie**.

When Ken tries to reinstitute patriarchy at a certain moment in the movie and then the women, inspired by Barbie and Gloria and Sasha, take over and change the constitution, there's this big moment where Ken wakes up and they have this heart-to-heart talk, Barbie and Ken.

Barbie says to him, "What are you doing?" **He says to her, "I thought this would be our house,"** meaning I thought there's a love story, we'd have a house together. She says, "I think I owe you an apology. Not every night has to be girl's night."

So we think she might be coming towards him? Oh, maybe she's recognizing that there *is* actually a love story?

So he leans over to kiss her, and she says, "No, no, no!" Meaning: *There's no Eros. There's no LoveDesire. That's not real.*

Then Ken says, "But I don't know who I am without you." And Barbie says, "You're Ken."

Now we'd like her to think, "Oh, go individuate and be Ken and come back to me." But that's exactly not what she means.

What she says is, "You actually are Ken, and I am Barbie, and there's no intrinsic allurement between us. There's no love story."

Then Ken says, "But I only exist within the warmth of your gaze."

Ken gets it. In the beginning of the movie, the movie opens with the narrator saying, "Barbie has a good day every day. Ken only has a good day if Barbie looks at him."

So they're mocking Ken, but it's actually Ken who in the entire movie holds the love story. But Ken in the movie is presented as corrupt patriarchy.

So what the movie has done—which is shocking—is it said, **there's no love story, there's no Barbie and Ken.**

That's the exact opposite of the realization in the interior and exterior sciences of the CosmoErotic Universe, which are saying it's "Barbie and Ken" all the way up and all the way down the evolutionary chain.

Reality is Barbie and Ken:

- Whether it's molecules coming together to form a macromolecule
- Whether it's your body and the cellular structure of your body, in which your body is a dazzling love story
- Whether it's the movement and allurement of the celestial bodies and the movement of gravity
- Whether it's the Eros that animates electromagnetism
- Whether it's protons, neutrons, and electrons becoming an atom

As Meister Eckhart, the Christian mystic, said: *Reality is kissing* all the way up and all the way down.

The four forces—gravity, electromagnetism, the strong and the weak nuclear—they are the forces of Eros, allurement, and autonomy.

No, no, no, postmodernism says through *Barbie: There is no Barbie and Ken.*

The only person who actually honors *LoveDesire* is Ken. We're making up a new word here, not love or desire, but *LoveDesire*, one word.

Scene 4: "I'm Just Ken"—*Allurement as a Strategy Of Patriarchy*

So the only person who honors LoveDesire is Ken, and he has a song, "I'm Just Ken," that he sings. He says in the song, "I have feelings I can't explain. They're driving me insane. Where I see love, she sees a friend. Is it my destiny to live and die a life of blonde fragility?"

And then he says one more line: "I want to know what it's like to love, to be the real thing. Is it a crime? Am I not hot when I'm in my feelings?"

So this is Ken standing for the love story. But who's Ken in the movie? A blithering idiot. He is degraded patriarchy in the movie.

So in this movie—that became the biggest box office hit, playing in theaters as *jihad* enters Israel in this tragic moment—**the basic point to the movie is:**

- There is no love story because there's no Field of Value in Cosmos.
- There's no Field of Eros, because Eros is not a value of Cosmos.
- The entire thing is completely made up.

The only people who think there's a love story are people who are using love for power, which is degraded patriarchy.

Scene 5: "Closer to Fine"—*There Is No Intrinsic Value In Cosmos*

The song by Indigo Girls, "Closer to Fine", appears three times in the movie. It's also in the trailer of the movie. So what's the song *Closer to Fine* about? It's about one thing. There's no love story. There's no Story of Value. It's not real. The actual refrain of the song is, "I went to the doctor, I went to the mountain, I looked to the children, I drank from the fountains." And then what happened? "There's more than one answer to these questions, pointing me in a crooked line." And the song says, actually: **"The less I seek my source for some definitive, the closer I am to fine."**

And *some definitive* means, something that's real, that's not created, that's not made up.

That song plays three times, and the point is: I'm *closer to fine* when I give up the Field of Value, when I give up the Field of Eros, when I give up the fact that I'm an expression and participate in The Universe: A Love Story.

Scene 6: *"Why Would You Want to Become Human"*

Finally, you have Ruth Handler talking to Barbie. She says to Barbie, who wants to become human, she's like, *Wow, that's a surprise. Why would you want to become human?*

Ruth says, "Humans basically make up meaning and they die. Why would you want to do that?"

Barbie, being a good existentialist, basically says, *Well, I'd like to participate in that social construction of meaning because it's very beautiful.*

But actually, there is no real meaning and there is therefore no real Eros, and there is no ErosValue, and the universe is not a love story.

So that's shocking.

AUBREY: EMPIRE WANTS TO CONTROL LOVE

What would you say about this read that just occurs to me as I'm thinking about it?

I read this as a transhumanist empire, fantasy, where empire is actually a projection of the ego, which wants to know itself in relative position to everybody else and be dominant in that relative position, which is why all of the dictators of all communist revolutions like Mao or Stalin, it's like, "Everybody's equal except for me. Except for me! I'm at the *fucking* top, and I can do whatever I want, and I'm in control of everything, and I'm the most powerful. Let's make a bunch of *fucking* statues of me and have people read books about me. Me, me, me!" And it's this complete absolute, like, "I am the father of all people and everybody else is beneath me."

There's this kind of idea, as empire is making its move to create this totalizing hierarchy, where there's going to be elites, which will eventually battle themselves, until there's one final elite that's at the very top of the pyramid, because multiple elites, they may share the ring of power for a while, but they'll all fight each other. It's in all the stories of culture. **Elites will all fight each other for the absolute ring of power until there's one Sauron.** There's one Mao. There's one Stalin. There's one Hitler. There's one person at the top.

There's also this movement that says, "Well, let's *decontextualize* and *de-eroticize* the world," and actually these dolls are a creation of a corporation, which ultimately is kind of like an embodiment of this entity of total control power. A corporation wants to make as much money as possible, swallow up as many other competitors as possible until they're at the very top.

These things seem to be connected, the totalizing empire and this kind of postmodern agenda to de-eroticize love. I forgot who said this beautiful quote, that *empire wants to control love.* **Empire wants to control love or totalitarianism wants to control love, because love is something they can't control.**

So if you create dolls with no genitals, and that's the whole creation of the thing, then you can be at the very top of everything, and there's no one who will have the energy, the *Fuck,* to actually challenge you.

Which is also why Mao, in the communist revolution, made all of the women dress like boys, cut off all of their hair, de-eroticized the whole body politic of all the citizens. Wipe out as many as possible, and then create this totalizing control, which is also cutting off people's love. Not only between each other, but **cutting off people's love for the Divine,** until all that there is left to love is the person at the top, which is the dictator, which is the tyrant.

MARC: LOVE IS REVOLUTIONARY

That is beautiful and important. So let's just unpack. You said a lot there. It's so important in terms of how we live our lives.

So one, love is revolutionary by its nature. Love is subversive. Love is by its nature subversive.

To say even very simply, *rivalrous conflict is governed by win -lose metrics.*

In that win-love metrics structure, everything is about: You're either giving or you're receiving. You're putting money in the bank, or you're taking money out.

Love undermines that.

When you're in the throes of LoveDesire, the split between giving and receiving disappears and giving and receiving become one.

So love undermines the win/lose metrics.

What does love mean? **Love means I'm willing to bracket my egoic self for a moment to be in devotion to your transformation, to your growth.** That's what it means to love. It means I bracket the win/lose metrics and I'm in devotion. I'm madly excited about Aubrey-ness and I don't view Aubrey-ness as an instrument to Marc-ness. That is what love means.

Love brackets the movement of empire.

Love brackets the win/lose metrics.

Love is subversive.

Love is revolutionary.

So by definition, love stands against empire.

It stands against the win/lose metrics.

It stands against this notion that there's a particular conspiracy theory: it's not that there is a *cabal* necessarily. **It's actually this false idea that the very structure of Reality is a structure of win/lose metrics.** It's a structure of a kind of anti-erotic, non-intimate universe.

Now that's why George Orwell in his book *1984* places the Ministry of Love at the center of the empire's totalitarianism. The entire point of *1984* is that we're going to break the love story between Winston and Julia. That's the entire point.

If we can break that ultimate love story, then actually, and tragically, *Moloch* wins. *Moloch* meaning that idolatrous force that Allen Ginsburg talked about in his poem *Howl*. He described reality as *Moloch*, the structure of the win/lose metrics, the structure of the absurd.

B.F. Skinner, who's the informative force defining the entire tech plex,[31] describes a city called Walden Two, in his book *Walden Two*. He's responding to Thoreau's *Walden,* which is about self-reliance and love and community—autonomy and communion all together. Skinner says in *Walden Two,* "No, actually, love's not real." In other words, *you create simulations of love*

---

31 By tech plex, we mean the technological infrastructure of society, which includes the entire planetary stack (Benjamin Bratton's term), as well as the daily immersive environment constituted by social media and the Internet of Things. The tech plex is unique in that it has facilitated a new world in which technology is no longer a tool, but an immersive environment. We live inside of that plex. That plex moves all the way up and all the way down the planetary stack. The tech plex is constituted by infrastructure, social structure, and superstructure, as we have previously defined these terms. Clearly, there's infrastructure, in terms of the actual physical structures of the tech plex. There's social structure, in relationship to the laws that govern and the absence of laws in relationship to the tech plex. And third, there's superstructure. That is to say, the technology actually codifies particular values and ignores, bypasses, or rejects other values. That is to say, the tech plex is not value-neutral; the tech plex implies a set of worldviews or superstructures.

like Barbie dolls, and you can actually commodify love, but it's controlled. It's not actually a true force.

The actual assumption of the mainstream intelligentsia that dominates the Western Academy is that actually *love is not real, value is not real,* and *there's no Barbie and Ken.*

So therefore, the revolution starts with the reclaiming of a love story.

You can't actually respond to the meta-crisis without reclaiming the love story, because **the meta-crisis at its core is two things:**

- It's rivalrous conflict governed by **win/lose metrics**, meaning that there's always win/lose metrics. There's never a love story.
- **It's what we call a fragile system.** In Nassim Taleb's research, a fragile system means a system where the parts don't *know* each other. The way we say this in the new Story of Value and Cosmo-Erotic Humanism is: where the parts aren't *allured* to each other. Since the parts aren't allured to each other, the system is fragile.[32]

Love is anti-fragile.

Love or *Fuck* is *unfuckable.*

That's its nature.

Reality is a love story.

Reality is an Intimate Universe.

That intimacy literally lives in me.

It's not just that I live in the Intimate Universe; the Intimate Universe lives in me.

That's true atomically, molecularly, neuronally—in my nerve endings, in my microbiome. Seventy percent of my immune system lives in my

---

32 For a deeper understanding of complex vs complicated, fragile systems, see David J. Temple, *First Principles and First Values* (2024), 75.

microbiome, where there is complete intimacy between my microbiome and the larger environment, there's a complete larger, wider shared identity.

Unless I begin to realize this and see that the whole thing is a love story, people are atomized against each other. Pseudo-eros, surface fulfillments of grasping and seeking, dominate the day, devising a world marked of mental breakdown, incoherence, and intense loneliness. If love is not real, loneliness can never be overcome.

If the world is not a love story, if there's no Field of Value or no Field of Eros, then loneliness can never be overcome.

MARC: TOTALITARIANISM SEEKS TO UNDERMINE LOVEDESIRE

It's not just love we're talking about, it's *LoveDesire*.

I think what you're pointing to, Aubrey, is that totalitarianism seeks to undermine *LoveDesire*.

- Number one, Barbie and Ken aren't real.
- Number two, to the extent that they do exist, **they have no genitals,** meaning the corporation has actually deconstructed any Reality to desire, because desire is subversive.

Desire means that Divinity courses in my body. There is dignity to desire. I feel the aliveness of my body. I feel that **the bill of rights is encrypted in my body-sacred.** I know that to touch, to arouse, is this enormous power I have.

Desire democratizes power, because desire is the power to give and receive pleasure as the self-evident value, in which I realize that I am a king and a queen.

Whenever I come together with my beloved, I am both king and queen, yet I am always, in my infinite, *She*-ness, *God-ness*, which is why at a moment of orgasm, we cry out, "Oh God!"

Totalitarianism, therefore, has to actually come in between me and my body. The body *is* a love story—literally, molecularly. We said earlier, atomically, the body is literally, in all of its structures, a love story. **So totalitarianism has to come in between me and my capacity to trust my desire, to trust my body.**

When totalitarianism can break my capacity to trust my body, I lose the self-authorship and the authority over the depth of my own desire. And we're not talking about surface desire, we're talking about my ability to actually clarify my desire, to access my deepest heart's desire.

My deepest heart's desire is what stands against empire.

Intimate communion between people gathering stands against empire.

AUBREY: EMPIRE'S DEGRADATION OF LOVE AWAKENS THE EROS OF THE WARRIOR

Let's look at another movie from culture. Movies speak. There's countless examples of this, but I'm going to talk about one.

In *Braveheart,* there is William Wallace, under the yoke of Edward Longshanks, who is a ruthless British Emperor. He is really a king, but he is acting as an emperor. We use *king* in a positive connotation, but he's the king as emperor, trying to control everyone, trying to control Scotland. William Wallace, a powerful warrior, filled with *Fuck*, filled with not only what you call *LoveDesire,* but also a sense of goodness.

He was actually happy to have a small cottage somewhere, maybe out in the glade, and raise a couple kids, but then empire presses a little too close. They try to rape his beloved. He goes on a little rampage and they try to escape, but they catch Murron, his beloved, who he just married in the secret glade. They have this scene where he takes off her cloak, as he's naked and she's naked, his hot breath is on her neck and you just feel her body open and quiver with the tenderness of this passionate lovemaking that's about to occur to consummate their marriage and you see this *LoveDesire* fill him. He was happy to lay down his sword. He was the wildly trained strategist, a technician warrior, but he was happy to just say, "It's okay. The empire has this; I'm going to carve out my little love story."

But then the empire pushes too close and they kill his beloved, and William Wallace is no longer just William Wallace. He becomes a hero—like a real hero. **When empire pushes too far, it awakens the lions, it awakens the dragons**. It awakens the inner warrior hero, that lives inside us.

I think it's why I always get emotional watching these movies because if we have the love story in the private, personal, we can kind of say, "Ah, it's okay, the world is kind of tough." **But the moment that the empire presses a little too close—however that is—it awakens something within somebody.**

Sometimes it's not even the romantic love story. I mean, look at the whole *John Wick* series. The empire fucked up. They made a mistake. He buried his guns. He was living in a house. He just loved his dog. They fucked up. They killed his dog. Then four movies later, and five hundred headshots, and the absolute destruction of this oppressive control of empire through this assassin's community—they just unleashed hell.

It is the same as what Longshanks and the British Empire did when they pressed against Wallace. We know this is true.

If they were actually able to degrade love itself, they wouldn't awaken the warriors.

But if they don't succeed in degrading love, then they're going to continue to awaken the warriors, the Lions of Judah, the William Wallaces, even the John Wicks.

MARC: THE FUNDAMENTALIST DESTRUCTION OF THE LOVE STORY

That's beautiful. In that sense, culture, the love story, speaks through John Wick, speaks through William Wallace, speaks through the great love story of Aragorn and Arwen in Tolkien's *Lord of the Rings*. The love story is going to animate and change the destiny of history.

Let's use the word *empire* for kind of the machinery of un-love, the machinery of the non-intimate universe. Empire makes a far more insidious move than Longshanks—which is *Barbie*.

Barbie is actually not innocent. You actually have a slightly chilled feeling when you leave the movie.

It's the same feeling you have when you finish reading Yuval Harari, who wrote a book called *Sapiens*. The basic point of the book is that there's this big story, but there's no love story. That Eros and value are not a quality of Cosmos. That there is no Field of Value and there is no Field of Eros, which is ErosValue, which is goodness.

But actually, goodness and love are one. There's no split between goodness and love. They're precisely the same. Eros is *right relationship*, it's the right ethos between parts.

So when you finish reading Harari's book, *Sapiens*, you have the same chilled feeling, you're not quite sure why you're uncomfortable and you have a sense of *ennui*, as Steiner put it, the sense that something has been deconstructed, that the world is not all right.

That is actually devastating, just as *Barbie* is.

I must have asked a hundred people in the last three months:

"How did you feel when you left the movie?"

"Funny..."

There's this insertion of a kind of parasitic virus that seeks to deconstruct the love story itself. That's the deconstruction of the love story. That's fundamentalism.

BARBIE AND HAMAS ARE FAILED LOVE STORIES THAT GENERATE EVIL

Now *jihad,* in its expression as ISIS or as Hamas, is actually also a failed love story.

Here the failed love story is:

- **Number one: Desire is evil.** That's the first thing. Desire is evil. That's critical. The experience of desire is evil. The experience of desire is about the dignity of the human body as this living, breathing, pulsing, throbbing expression of desire. So in the failed love story of *jihad,* desire itself is evil. That's number one.
- **Number two, there's no Field of Eros, which is a Field of Value, in which all of Reality participates.** In every human being, in all of the animal world, and in all the atomic world—there's no shared Field of Desire. There's not even a shared Field of Desire and Eros and value between human beings. There's a line that splits Reality. It's *Dar al-Harb* and *Dar al-Islam.* There's those who should be put to death by the line of the sword, and there is a very small, narrow group of people—we're not sure, are they Sunnis, are they Shias—a very tiny group, only they are beloved of God.

So *jihad* is an abusive love story, where those involved abuse the body, because the body is not considered a place that is sacred. This bypasses the dignity of the body, which is why there are high rates of incest, honor killings, and abuse within that kind of fundamentalist culture. The body has no dignity. Desire has no dignity.

When desire has no dignity, and everyone else is seen as the people who should be destroyed by the sword, it means there is no Field of ErosValue.

So imagine, within this framework, you're now experiencing desire in yourself. What do you do with that? You project desire, which is evil, onto the other, and then you torture them. Torture is the inverse of the love story.

In other words, when there's no love story, when there's no Field of ErosValue, you don't caress, you don't make love, you don't arouse.

The opposite of LoveDesire is literally torture.

So when I'm a young Hamas man and I experience desire, it's seen as evil. I then project this sense of evil living in my body onto the other—the *other* is anyone outside my inner circle. From there, I don't just seek to kill them; I seek to dismember them.

We have, even the United Nations now has, more forensic evidence of brutality on October 7 of cutting off limbs while raping someone, and then shooting them, and then continuing to rape them.

This is not happening naturally. Actually all the Hamas boys, the ISIS boys, **were jacked up on amphetamines, which turned off the love story of the body**. It jacked up the aggressive centers and completely depressed or turned off the centers of love and empathy in the body. **So they literally turned off the love story in the body. They lived in an anti-erotic story, a story which violates intimacy.** Then they exploded in the tragedy of *jihad* and atrocity—because it's a failed love story.

But we have to understand they're not actually *intrinsically* evil devils, aka Zoroastrianism; that they're not actually of Ahura Mazda; they're not actually of *the other side*.

No, they're actually part of the love story. They're part of the Field of Eros, which is why they have to take those amphetamines, which is why it's a failed love story that turns them to evil.

So on the Hamas side, it's a failed story of the dignity of desire. A failed love story which is ethnocentric, meaning only those inside of my circle are deserving of love—and the body is not a love story. That's what produces atrocity on the side of Hamas.

On the other side, *Barbie* is a failed love story as well. Love is commodified, owned.

Whether it's Skinner in *Walden Two*, who talks about creating a community in which love is controlled and contrived and commodified—it's not real—or whether it's Orwell, who talks about the Ministry of Love in *1984*, or whether it's Barbie who says there's no Barbie and Ken, they're all saying the same thing:

We're going to control Reality, and we're going to do that by actually saying, "There's no dignity to desire; there's no love story; there's no *LoveDesire*."

So strangely and paradoxically, these two sides of the world both generate evil: the postmodern deconstruction as expressed in Barbie, which animates Moloch or empire, on the one hand, and on the other hand, the tragic Hamas culture of death, which is anti-life.

They both generate evil of completely different forms over time, but **they're expressions of evil because they're failed love stories.**

That is actually hopeful. That's the thing. That's actually hopeful.

It's hopeful because the love story is real and it can be re-aroused, but we have to tell a new story and show it to be true. Wow!

AUBREY: THE FALLEN ANGEL WANTS TO GET BACK TO ONE LOVE THROUGH DESTRUCTION

I'm going to open up something that we won't get to fully conclude in this conversation. Marc, we've had a beautiful conversation about this before.

As I look at the Cosmos, as I've come to understand it through my *psychonautics*, the One splits into two opposing forces, but it's all the One which is the love story, which is *Shekhinah,* which is the Divine, which is the Tao, which is the Mystery. **It is all a love story.**

But then there's a split into polarity, life and anti-life. You could split it in a bunch of different ways. There is an intending non-planetary, extra-dimensional force that is not God, but it is a demon— a demonic force. I think there's also a place where people can be in a love story with this demonic force, where they're actually in active, devotional worship of death, for this culture of death, for this culture of anti-life. There can be a pleasure in worshiping this demon.

I've explored this since our earlier conversation Marc, and what I see is that actually, that force is still a part of the love story. I actually saw the One split into polarity in a psychedelic medicine journey.

I saw it happening as a wobble where the One just started to wobble and created this sine wave of peaks and valleys. In the sine wave, which is the ups and downs, polarity was created. There was the top, there was a peak and there was the bottom.

As it split, that force on the dark side, on the downswing, let's call it, actually has the same impulse to return to love, which is absolute unification. **So it has this desire to return to love.** But it fails to be able to do that, because it's locked in polarity.

So if you go down the dimensional Cosmos, you start going down to the seventh dimension, which is where these extra dimensional forces actually live.

They actually are trying to destroy everything because in the destruction of all creation and everything, there'll be the void, which is Oneness, which is back to unification, with love.

So the idea of the fallen angel, really the fallen angel just says, "I want to get back to the house of God, of Love. So my way to do that is by actually destroying everything."

Whereas the other force says, "No, no, no, let's create all unique, intimate possibilities and return to unification with love through the other side."

So even on these other sides, even though their intention may be pure destruction, they're still part of the love story.

So Ahura Mazda (the Zoroastrian one true god) and Angra Mainyu (Zoroastrian expression of evil and destruction) are still in this drive to actually return to the one love.

MARC: EVIL IS THE ANTI-LIFE FORCE

That's very beautiful. You're gorgeously weaving Ahura Mazda into the lineage of Solomon.

You're kind of overcoming the split in Zoroastrianism, and you're kind of reading it in a Solomonic lineage, which I think is a beautiful reading. I think you're absolutely right.

What you're saying is so beautifully true in terms of the essence of Reality.

To make it most personal and intimate:

Evil doesn't live out there, evil lives everywhere. Evil is the anti-life force.

It's the place when you're in the middle of an argument, which is fierce, and you just want to say, "*Fuck* you, I'm walking out. I'm not going to reach in and find the place where I have a part of this contribution system, and I'm just not climbing down from the *fucking* tree because I just won't do it."

The place where I won't bracket self, for the sake of feeling other, this mutuality of feeling, that is the root of evil.

You can't have your gun looking into a safe house in an Israeli kibbutz and see four children and shoot them in the belly and not be disconnected from your ability to feel the field.

So clearly, you've lost connection to the love story.

After the Hamas boy killed ten Jews, and as we heard on one of the recordings, the boy calls home and he asks his mother, "Are you proud of me?"

That requires from us to hold this very, very painful, poignant, fierce paradox. Meaning, **we have to act and make war for peace. Just like we make love for peace. We sometimes have to make war for peace.** That's what we had to do in response to Nazism. We can't actually allow atrocity to stand. At the same time we remember that Germany did transform itself. Even in the anti-love story of Hamas, the son of Hamas, Mosab Hassan Yousef, found his way and actually became a hero. His story was told in the documentary about his life called "The Green Prince."

There's no Hamas boy or Hamas woman who ultimately, in the arc of history, can't actually find their way back to the love story.

And in this moment right now, we actually have to do what needs to be done, to stand for love with full fierceness. William Wallace had to do what William Wallace had to do for the sake of love. So it requires from us this intense and stunning and infinitely painful and poignant paradox: **to wield the sword fiercely for the sake of love.** That's actually what needs to be done. The allies needed to do that in World War II. When Tom Hanks made *Saving Private Ryan*, and those boys swept the beaches of Normandy, those boys had **a sacred impulse of love animating their hearts.**

No one's ever ultimately out of the story. No demon doesn't find their way back. Even the orcs in Tolkien, in the *Lord of the Rings*, the orcs who were originally elves, who had fallen.

There's always a way home. Sometimes it's in this incarnation, and sometimes it's in the next incarnation. Which is why we always have to hold this widest love story and act fiercely for it.

Right now, the most revolutionary act we can do is to actually tell a new story. Just like five hundred years ago, a bunch of people got together in Florence and they told this new story. Democracy was a joke a thousand years ago. And all of a sudden, you have democracy and you have universal human rights, which is the movement of a love story.

Right now in this time between worlds, we can't go to Hamas. We can't go to the old religions. We can't go to a deconstructed postmodernism and *Barbie*.

So what we have to do is tell a new story—which brings together interior sciences and exterior sciences—which lives in us. A new story in which we have a direct experience that **our personal love story matters infinitely to the Cosmos, that our desire matters infinitely.**

We have to tell this new story, not a declared story, not a made-up story, but this grounded, gorgeous, stunning story of *LoveDesire*.

Every man, woman, and child needs to grow up and know that story and grow into that story.

This shift, this transformation, is a revolution of love—but again, not in a tinsel sense, not in a declared sense.

It's actually a new science.

It's a new neuro-dharma that needs to come together.

It's a great new Renaissance that needs to happen.

It's the overwhelming moral imperative of this moment.

It's the imperative of articulating and telling that new love story in a way that everyone has a place and everyone can come home.

AUBREY: ARTISTS REMIND US OF THE NATURE OF COSMOS

It seems like the control of access to this love story is what is actually preventing it. But in these cultures that deny the love story, you get the movements that happen, for example with Mahsa Amini versus the mullahs in Iran.

How does that happen? Despite the controls and the internet service providers trying to limit things and trying to keep this love story from speaking in culture, they still have access to these books and they have access to these ideas, and these ideas become subversive to the other fundamentalist totalitarian ideas. Unless they *degrade* the ideas in stories and culture, people will actually find them.

It's so important for the artists to keep singing love songs and for the storytellers and the movie makers to keep creating love stories that remind us of the nature of Cosmos itself.

The proliferation of these love stories is inevitable, unless we degrade the story itself sufficiently. Whether it's *Barbie* or whether it's the movie *Everything Everywhere All At Once*, where the only actual love is found in these tiny little moments that are completely inconsequential because the universe is random and chaotic and nothing is actually real, because every possibility exists. So there is no plotline, whatsoever. You can have giant dildo fingers or be all warped out. Nothing actually makes sense anyways.

MARC: MY STORY HAS TO BECOME PART OF THE LOVE STORY OF THE WHOLE

In *Everything Everywhere All At Once* there's no plotline. That's the sense. There's no plotline.

The word *love* and *story* go together ontologically.

Love is a story.

Love is a love story.

Reality is not just love.

Reality is a love story.

When we actually find the inner thread of our lives, our lives are a sacred autobiography, they're a story, and that story is honored by *She*.

William Wallace understands that if you violate my private love story, you violate the Cosmos. But my private love story is not just me. **My private love story has to expand and get deeper and wider, and has to become the love story of the whole.**

So we need actually to reclaim the evolutionary realization that Reality is *LoveDesire,* and *LoveIntelligence,* and *LoveBeauty*—from its atomic, to its cellular, to its biological, to its cultural level. That's actually the nature of Reality.

So for example, if I'm sitting here and watching Aubrey right now, how do I participate in the revolution? I deepen my love story. That's where I start. **The revolutionary act is to become a lover in a deeper way, to expand my love, and to deepen**—to deepen where I am and to expand, that's the act of revolution.

We can't even begin that conversation unless we transcend, we end the trance of *jihad,* and we end the trance of *Barbie,* which are both failed love stories. Because that's how we began.

206

A failed love story equals evil.

In the battle between good and evil, the essential move of good now is to tell a new story. Because it's actually the best story that wins. But it's not the best because it's simply the best; it's the best because it's the most compelling, the most alive, the most alluring—because it is most aligned with the nature of the real in which we participate, so we recognize its truth. It's the best story that wins.

AUBREY: WIELDING THE SWORD OF PEACE

The best story is a love story. It's what moves us the most in every way. You know what I mean?

No matter what we have to do in this world, how we wield the sword—my mythical sword. I love fantasy lore. My mythical sword, I call it *War's Bane*, the *Bane of War*. It's **a sharp sword, but its purpose is peace.** Its purpose is peace, the purpose is love. It's the *Bane of War*.

It's the force that is standing for that. I think that story is the most compelling story, unless we can actually universally *degrade* the love story—and there are clearly forces trying to do that. But unless it's completely *degraded* and we all lose the plot together, **the lions, the heroes, the dragons, they're actually going to awaken.**

I think that's what's happening here. **Despite all of the pain and suffering**—which is all extremely real on Israel's side, on Palestine's side, and on the side of all of the world that's suffering, all the children who are sex trafficked, and all of the horrors that exist—**there's still the best story that will ultimately triumph.**

I really believe that.

We just have to stay alive and not destroy ourselves while we've lost the plot. We have to get the plot back with enough time for that story to win.

Marc: That is gorgeous, my friend. Last sentence, from me to you, my heart to your heart. *Hanukkah* is a holy day in the lineage of Solomon, which is about a little bit of light that dispels a lot of darkness.

We need to take back holy days and we need to create this hope, as you say it, because hope is always a memory of the love that's yet to come.

Aubrey: Beautiful. Beautiful. All in for all life, my brother.

Marc: All in for all life, my brother. Love you mad.

CHAPTER 13

BARBIE, HAMAS & *HOMO AMOR*—FROM DEGRADED LOVE STORIES TO THE UNIVERSE: A LOVE STORY

INTRODUCTION

In the previous chapters, we began to look at two seemingly unconnected events—the *Barbie* movie and the Hamas atrocities of October 7, 2023—which helps us clarify our perception and articulate a third possibility.

Although there is zero moral equivalence between *Barbie* and Hamas, **both are degraded love stories.** That's what makes them so dangerous.

- Hamas is a wildly destructive expression of fundamentalism ; it degrades and demonizes the body and desire itself. Desire, perceived as evil, is projected outwards, onto "infidels," and then brutally destroyed.

209

- *Barbie* is an expression of postmodernism: it disqualifies love, value, and desire as non-real, as mere social constructs.

In absence of real value, we lose capacity for moral distinctions; that's how Hamas atrocities could escape condemnation or even be celebrated on university campuses across the Western world.

Postmodernism and fundamentalism are swelling movements in today's world, and both will destroy us.

Our only chance is the third way, the third possibility—articulating a shared Story of Value rooted in the clarified realization that the Universe *is* a love story,

Reality *is* desire, and no one is excluded from the love story.

WE NEED TO FIND A THIRD WAY

We need to clear our glasses. We need to be able to see clearly. *Homo amor* needs to be able to clear our glasses, to clarify the interior, to be able to stand in love, to be able to stand in Eros.

If you've tracked and understood the fabric of interior culture, the confusion is not surprising. But sometimes something can be *not* surprising, but *shocking*.

The confusion lies in the incapacity to distinguish between:

- The utter tragedy of innocent civilians being killed in Gaza—or anyplace in the world, which rips our hearts out—and the *jihadi* culture of death.
- **A culture of *death* and a culture of *life*—**one which may have a thousand problems, but is fundamentally a culture of life.

This incapacity to make distinctions, undermines the capacity to be *Homo amor*.

We need to be able to make these distinctions.

The first requirement of *Homo amor* is that we feel the joy. We feel the pulsing joy of the world, and when there is pain, we feel the pulsing pain of the world.

No one's blood is cheap. Ukrainian blood is not cheap, and Yemeni blood is not cheap, and Jewish blood is not cheap, and Palestinian blood is not cheap. All blood has the same value, the same intrinsic value. No one's blood is cheap.

And we need to be able to make the fundamental distinction between a *jihadi* culture of death and an—at least aspiring—culture of life that needs to respond to it.

In order to be able to respond to the culture of death we have to first understand it, and then we need to embrace a new Story of Value.

From where we stand today, we don't have the capacity, as *Homo amor,* to respond to the culture of death.

I'm going to be as precise as I can and outline the movie *Barbie,* the atrocities committed by *Hamas,* and the new story. Those are the three options we have for the world today.

- *Barbie,* as we'll see, will lead to a nihilistic destruction.
- *Hamas* will lead to a puritanical destruction.
- **Only a new Story of Value**—which realizes that the Universe is a love story, that I participate in that love story, and that no one is outside the circle—**can actually *respond* and move us from horror to hope.**

That realization is based not simply on *declaration,* but on a careful reading of both the hard, exterior sciences and what I would call *the interior sciences,* the wisdom traditions.

- It's *only* such a realization
- It's *only* such an evolution of culture and consciousness
- It's *only* such a progression of moral grasp and understanding

- It's *only* such a progression of ethos rooted in a realization of *Eros*

—that can respond to the culture of death and create the new world, the most beautiful world that we've always known is possible.

The refusal to make distinctions contravenes the interior of *Homo amor.*

Love is not merely a feeling, love is a perception. But this does not mean I have stopped feeling. I feel insanely. I am by nature an empath, so I feel all the time; I'm always feeling. I have never, quite literally never, had a good idea in my life. Any idea, any *dharma,* any set of distinctions that I am trying to articulate comes from a deep feeling, a felt sense—and I try to articulate the feeling as it stays with me. Day in and day out, I try and articulate the feeling, and then share it. I am trying to share a *feeling,* and then to articulate it in a *distinction.*

We have to *feel.* It's only our capacity *to feel and articulate* this new Story of Value that can allow us to move from horror to hope, to the hope which is a memory of the future.

Evolutionary Love Code

There are three Universe Stories.

There is the Barbie Universe Story.

There is the Hamas Universe Story, the fundamentalist Universe Story (there are different forms of fundamentalism).

And then there is the *Homo amor,* CosmoErotic Humanism story, the new Story of Value.

Those are the three choices that we have today. It's not a binary choice; we need to find a third way. We need to find our way between the binary of Barbie and Hamas—between postmodern, desiccated, empty materialism, and a pseudo-erotic fundamentalism, which is wildly destructive.

The third way is the new Story of Value rooted in evolving First Principles and First Values, CosmoErotic Humanism.

FALSE STORIES CONFUSE US

Stories *matter*.

Story is the very structure of Reality itself.
Story is not a human invention.
Story is ontological to Cosmos.

In interior sciences, there is a phrase we sometimes use: *God loves stories*. That's another way of talking about story as structural to Reality.

Don't worry if you're confused about God. As we often say, the god you don't believe in doesn't exist, it's okay. The god that you deny, I deny also. When we talk about God, we mean the Field of Value that is infinitely personal.

In CosmoErotic Humanism, we have a name that we use to refer to the Divine that both *lives in us* and *holds us*, and that name is the Infinite Intimate. God is the Infinite Intimate. The Infinite that desires intimacy, and becomes somehow paradoxically *more* infinite through desiring intimacy and through realizing ever deeper intimacies.

Why does that matter so insanely much in this very moment?

False stories confuse us.

I'll give you an example of a false story.

The atrocity of October 7th took place because of the interior logic of Hamas, which is a failed love story. In the previous chapters we talked about Hamas as a failed love story.

It has nothing to do with "the occupation of Gaza," whatever *the occupation* means. That word doesn't even *mean* anything, it's an overused trope, *the occupation of Gaza*. Who is occupying Gaza, what does it even mean? Where is Gaza? When was it part of Egypt? Israel unilaterally withdrew from Gaza. Hamas took it over, threw out Fatah, and basically massacres and kills its citizens at will in order to hold them captive for its own *jihadi* aims. **Whenever someone says *the occupation of Gaza*, they actually don't know what they are referring to, and have no sense of the storyline.**

I'll give you a better piece of evidence. If you study the history of the Islamic State, or ISIS, in Iraq and in Syria, there was no occupation there—no West Bank, no Israel, no Jews, no occupation—and still, the Islamic State acted with barbarity and cruelty and atrocity of the same nature.

Or if you see the movie, *Hotel Mumbai*, which is about another *jihadi* set of atrocities that killed around 160 people. Again, there is no Israel there, and no occupation, and no Zionist entity—none of those smokescreens. And *jihad* does what *jihad* does.

That's really critical to understand. It is very clear that Hamas, although quite distinct from ISIS, is operating in the fundamental logic of a culture of death.

We're going to go much deeper than that. That's just the very beginning. But clearly, it's not about an occupation.

First, because the word *occupation* doesn't make sense in the Gaza context.

Secondly, how do you know the difference between a reason and an excuse? If you remove the excuse, does the phenomenon still exist? That's a very good distinction.

If the reason for Hamas's atrocities is presented as a response to a political agenda opposed by Israel, then consider this: if you remove Israel, remove Jews, or remove any of those specific factors—would *jihadism* still carry out its atrocities? The answer is *Yes*.

Whatever the political sets of issues are in Gaza or the West Bank, they are not the cause. By the way, according to all current polls, Hamas would win an election in the West Bank; let's just keep that in mind.

Someone could say: "But this is not *jihad*, it's pseudo-jihad. What *jihad* really means is an internal struggle for liberation."

The most important thing that could happen in the world today would be that the interpretation of *jihad* as an *internal struggle for liberation* would be accepted.

That would be the most beautiful, gorgeous evolution. We need two billion Muslims to arise in the world and say, "what *jihad* means is internal transformation." *Amen, Hallelujah*! That is what needs to happen. **We need an evolution of consciousness within Islam.**

But that has not happened.

Instead, if you read the classical interpretations that are dominating the discourse, *jihad* is *very centrally* about violence and war, with Muhammad as the model. That is their interpretation of *jihad* that they're now enacting. We need an evolution of what *jihad* means, and that would be probably one of the most pivotal evolutions of consciousness that we could enact.

A FAILED LOVE STORY ON A COLLECTIVE LEVEL RESULTS IN HORROR

But let's go deeper. This is just the surface, we're just on the surface now.

Hamas is not a group of sociopaths.

It's critical to understand, Hamas are not sociopaths. They're not psychopaths. There might be a random sociopath and psychopath, and there may be more than a few, like there always is. But if Hamas was just basically a group of mafia sociopaths, we would have a much smaller problem.

No, the whole point is that Hamas are ordinary people who are fundamentally psychologically sound, who have been completely absorbed in a failed love story. The acts they carry out are an expression of an utterly distorted version of a love story. **It's an utter degradation of a love story.**

That's the point.

That's what we see when we listen to an audio that was published online of a young man named Muhammed, who calls home and he says:

> "Dad, I killed ten with my bare hands! Dad, look at the WhatsApp and see how many I killed. Open Whatsapp and see how many I killed! I'm calling you from a mobile phone of a Jewish woman, I killed her and her husband. Dad, I killed ten! Their blood is on my hands. Mom, I killed more than 1ten Jews with my bare hands. Mom, your son is a hero. Kill, kill, kill! Please be proud of me dad!"

His father says, "You killed ten Jews?" And his mother is there crying. His father says: "Return to Gaza, return..." Muhammed says, "What shall I return to? My mother gave birth to me into this religion of Allah!" So there is a *shared conversation* between them.

Compare this to the My Lai massacre, where First Lieutenant Calley and his company commander Medina murdered at least 300 Vietnamese civilians at a small South Vietnamese sub-hamlet called My Lai. Can you imagine Calley and Medina calling home to Wyoming and Nebraska, and telling their parents: *Wow, I just killed 10 people!* The parents would be horrified. *You're out of your mind! What the fuck happened to you?* That's not what happens in this phone call. There is a culture of *jihad*. And the father says, *when are you going to come home?*

Martyrdom. Victory of martyrdom.

Clearly, martyrdom was where their son Muhammed was going. But Muhammed is not evil in the sense that he's expressing psychopathy, he is not. He is not a psychopath. He is not a sociopath. **He is a normal person with**

some elemental psychological soundness trapped in a failed love story, and this is far, far more dangerous.

Just ask former football player O.J. Simpson what it means to be trapped in a failed love story. O.J. Simpson is an example of failed love story on a personal level, which resulted in murder of his former wife and her friend.

But a failed love story on a collective level results in horror. In the fourteenth century, it resulted in the horrors of The Crusades, and on burning heretics alive, and flaying their skin. In the *jihadist* moment, it results in this ultimate violation of *Homo amor,* and the unimaginable atrocities of October 7th.

That's just our context. So the context is: *story matters.* **The story you tell matters.**

LET'S GET OUT OF SUPERFICIAL DISTORTIONS

We need to step out of the horror of social media feeds. They are so often utterly lost in the sad dimensions of human beings. Their architecture and their incentive structures are perverse, and they all too often reward the lowest common denominator of human expression. Let's get out of these social media feeds. Let's get out of this unimaginably superficial set of distortions, colored by any number of motivations, of the kind that existed in so much of the legacy press.

For example, some time ago, when a hospital was bombed, and Hamas immediately said, *Israel did this*, and Israel said, *we did not. The New York Times, BBC, Reuters,* and *The Guardian* all reported, based on Hamas, that Israel did it, without any checks or verification. It turned out, based on all the available intelligence in multiple vectors, not to be true. What caused our legacy press institutions to do that is a deeper conversation we're not going to have now.

Let's get out of those vectors, both out of the legacy press and out of the social media feeds, and let's look clearly, with our hearts wide open.

217

Our intention is to come to joy.

Our intention is the evolution of love.

Our intention is to clear our glasses, to see clearly.

BARBIE AS THE FIRST FAILED STORY OF DESIRE

Now let's return to **Barbie** and briefly recapitulate some of the core points we made in earlier chapters. Remember, **Barbie** was the movie that played in theaters in lots of the United States, just as the Hamas atrocities were happening.

This is culture telling a story. This is the Intimate Universe whispering.

What is *Barbie* saying? What is the *Barbie* story about?

Remember the scene at the end of the movie where Sasha, the daughter of Gloria, says, "What about Barbie? What's her ending? What does she get?" The head of Mattel says, "That's easy, she's in love with Ken!" But Barbie says, "I'm not in love with Ken."

If you follow the movie carefully, Barbie is not saying here *I'm not in love with **this** Ken*. This is not a *personal* Barbie and a *personal* Ken. Barbie and Ken here are archetypes. They are two parts in a larger system, and the question is, **is there a love story in the system or is there not?**

The entire point and plot of Barbie is that there is no love story.

That's why Barbie says to Ken, when he moves to kiss her in the beginning, "You can go now." And he says, "I thought I might stay over." She says, "Why?" *Why would you stay over?* "It's girls' night every night forever."

- Eternity is not about eternal love.
- Eternity is not about a love story.
- There *is* no love story.

Remember we carefully read the lyrics of the key songs in the movie, "Closer to Fine" and "I'm Just Ken," the point of the songs is: there is no love story. *Barbie is not in love with Ken* means: Barbie is not in love with any Ken, period. Love is *not* the end of the story. It's not where we're going.

It is not just a healthy individuation, which is how we would *like* to understand **Barbie**: Ken has to individuate, and Barbie has to individuate, and then they come together in this new Eros and this larger love. That's exactly *not* what **Barbie** is saying, if you read the text carefully. **Barbie says, there is no love story.**

Then we looked at this incredible scene where Barbie is talking to Ruth, Mrs. Handler, the founder of Mattel. Barbie says, *I want to become a human.* And Ruth says, *why?* She describes human beings and says, *and in the end, they die.*

Death, that's the end, it's over. They just make up meaning along the way, they just basically make shit up, because the whole thing is this fleeting thing, and why would you want to join that?

No answer to that question is given in *Barbie.*

It is very, very different from that moment in Tolkien, in *The Lord of the Rings* trilogy. Arwen, who is an eternal—or close to eternal—elf, decides she wants to become human even if she loses her eternity, in order to be with Aragorn. She wants to be with Aragorn because Reality *is* a love story, and because love is an eternal value of Reality itself—**so to step into love *is* to step into eternity.**

That's precisely *not* what's happening in *Barbie.*

Barbie is a world in which death ends life, in which after death, there is only nothingness. There is no Field of Value. Humans make it up, it's not real. Therefore the closest that Barbie can get to a love story is biological, so the relationship between Sasha and her mother is a love story. There are five or six scenes where that biological love story unfolds. Even Ruth says, "I named Barbie after my daughter, Barbara." It's all about the mother-daughter story, the feminine biological love story, because the masculine is demonized in Barbie. That's as close as we can get to a love story, but the core is **there is no love story, no Eros.** That's *Barbie*'s point.

There is no love story, because love itself is not a value, because Eros itself is not an intrinsic value of Cosmos.

You have a postmodern *desiccation*, as Lewis Mumford called it, a *disqualification of the universe*.

There is no Field of Value, and there is no ultimate distinction between right and wrong. That distinction can't be drawn. It's an arbitrary distinction.

As Yuval Harari basically says, there is no difference at all, in any ultimate sense, between massacring Muslims in the fourteenth century as a Christian young knight, and going to that same region of the world to work to help refugees for Amnesty International. He says quite explicitly, those are both just made-up stories, and in a few hundred years, the story we tell now, the Amnesty International story, the positive Western value story, will also seem absurd to us. There is no ultimate distinction.

I'm not citing Harari as a thinker. He's not important as a thinker. He's important as an uncontaminated and unconscious parrot of the *Barbie* predicament, which is that there is no love story.

When there is no Eros, there is *pseudo-eros*.

When there is no love story, all you get is the drive for power. All you get is rivalrous conflict governed by win/lose metrics. What you get is a war machine. You get a military-industrial complex, you get a medical-industrial complex.

You get the lowest common denominator of human drives, which are drives of *pseudo-eros*.

Eros is not just Eros.

Eros is the movement of separate parts desiring deeper contact and greater wholeness.

Eros = the experience of radical aliveness seeking, desiring ever deeper contact and ever greater wholeness.

This is the new story. In the new Universe Story, desire is real, it is a value of Cosmos. When you clarify desire, your clarified desire tells you what you value. Desire is an appropriate, and legitimate, and important compass. I **follow my clarified compass of desire in order to disclose value.**

Eros is a value. Eros is a value of Cosmos.

But if there is no Eros, then there is only emptiness. We try to fill it up, because we can't bear the emptiness. Postmodern materialism has no explanation of *why* we can't bear the emptiness. Existentialism describes—Sartre and Camus describe—with great grotesque detail, the experience of emptiness, but they ignore the question of *why* the emptiness is there. If we are but desiccated flatland, postmodern, mechanical humans, without any intrinsic value, then why do we feel this emptiness? They can't explain that.

If there is no Eros, there is pseudo-eros.

Pseudo-eros appears in many forms. One form of pseudo-eros is a military-industrial complex, this flexing of muscle, this drive to war, the war machine. Postmodernity can produce war machines, and war machines benefit from wars. Whenever there is a war, you'll always have to try and see where is the war machine? Where is the hidden war machine?

Postmodernity creates a moral vacuum. Moral vacuums benefit war machines that traffic in raw power. We all just have to be aware: is there a war machine someplace here, someplace in the background? We have to feel where the war machine is. Yet we have to keep in mind that not all war machines are the same, and there are wars that *need* to be fought, as I've talked about, as the Dalai Lama has talked about. Pacifism is not always an option, if I am taking responsibility for love, and if I am taking responsibility for the present, and for the future.

What emerges out of *Barbie* is a dogmatic claim that there is no love story—because there is no Field of Value, and therefore no ErosValue in Cosmos—**and so *pseudo-eros* goes to destroy everything** through its rivalrous conflict governed by win/lose metrics.

That's one story. In this story, desire is not a value of Cosmos. Desire is not sacred. I can't listen to my desire. My clarified desire means nothing. It is just the social construction that dominates who I am.

- There is no free choice.
- There is no choosing of direction.
- It's an illusion. It's made-up.
- My experience of freedom is dismissed, because my experience is dismissed.
- My desire for freedom is dismissed, because desire has no ontology. It has no Reality. It has no ultimate moral force.

That's the first story.

So what is *Barbie*? A failed love story. A failed story of desire.

HAMAS AS THE SECOND FAILED STORY OF DESIRE: THE DEMONIZATION AND DEGRADATION OF DESIRE

What is Hamas? In a completely different way, it's the same interior structure.

Obviously, there is *zero* moral equivalence between *Barbie* and Hamas, but in terms of its *interior structure*, Hamas is also a failed love story: there is no universal grammar of value rooted in Eros. There is no universal Field of Eros. Reality is divided in only one way. It's not divided between regions, or geographies, or nations, certainly not nation states. **It is divided in one way, *Dar Al Harb* and *Dar Al Islam:* those who should be brutally subjugated, and those who are purified by the only pure version of Islam.** Whether it's the *Sunni* version or the *Shia* version of *jihad* is a deathly argument between those versions of *jihad*, but what they share is that only a purified Islam is worthy of care and concern and love.

In this failed love story, the body is demonized. The stirrings of desire in the body are demonized. Masturbation has no place. Self-pleasuring has no place. The joy of making love, within the right and sacred context, has no place. That's critical: the body cannot be trusted. **The stirrings of desire in the body can't be trusted.**

Martyrdom, the rejection of the embodied manifest Reality is at the center of the conversation.

Now, if the body cannot be trusted, and I experience, deep in my body, the stirring of desire—in violation of the purified version of Islam which has animated my consciousness from early childhood—then I feel there is evil in me.

I cannot *own* that evil, so I project it outwards, on *the other*, on the enemy, on the infidel, who needs to be slaughtered by the sword, and painfully.

Anthony Blinken, the Secretary of State of the United States, reports on the atrocities committed on October 7th—a firsthand testimony about families being tied together. Children and parents, with the limbs of the children, fingers and legs, cut off. We're talking about phalluses of men cut off before their raped women, and then everyone burned alive.

This is what we're talking about. We're talking about this most torturous, most brutal, most vicious slaughter, to inflict the most pain possible. To cut a girl's arm off and leave her, without killing her, intentionally, so she'll wallow for seven hours in her pain. That's the intention. Then she quivers and dies in the end, as one of the first responders arrives hours later.

Because the experience of desire has been degraded.

Because desire is *not holy.*

Barbie, in its way, *disqualifies* desire:

- Desire is not real.
- Desire doesn't tell me anything real about Reality.
- DesireEros, desire which is the face of Eros, doesn't lead me to ethos.

In the Hamas version, desire is not just disqualified, but *degraded* *and demonized*, and therefore, the body can be violated. An anti-desire torture—the opposite of desire—is inflicted in the name of this purity.

The experience of interior desire, which is experienced as evil, is projected outwards—and then that desire is killed, and destroyed, and violated. That is the interior logic of the *jihadi* position. Not because they're sociopaths, not because they're psychopaths, but because that's what the good martyr does, inherently.

That's why even though the details of all these killings were known, they were often not condemned and were even *celebrated.*

But the atrocities were not condemned and were celebrated *on two different streets*:

- They were excused and even celebrated **on the postmodern street**, in universities across the world, including the best of Western liberal universities, who live in a postmodern predicament in which there is no Field of Value. When there is no Field of Value, you cannot do *evaluation.* If there's no Field of Value, you cannot evaluate anything. Evaluation makes distinction. We lose the capacity to make distinctions, which is where the false notion of *moral equivalence* has come from.

- They were celebrated **on the street in which *jihad* is celebrated**. Even if one is not an active *jihadi,* there is an enormous sympathy to *jihad* throughout huge swaths of Reality. There is this demonized degraded desire, which allows for an embrace of this *jihadi* worldview, which is then celebrated, in huge rallies around the world.

THE THIRD RESPONSE IS A NEW STORY OF VALUE

So what's the response? What's the third possibility?

A third possibility is a return to Eros.

But it is actually not *a return*—it is the articulation, *for the first time*, of the realization that the Universe is a love story.

In CosmoErotic Humanism we've stated that existential risk is *global* (climate change, artificial intelligence, the gap between haves and have-nots).

- Global challenges require **global solutions.**
- Global solutions require **global coordination.**
- Global coordination requires **global resonance,** or **global coherence.** We need global coherence in order to resonate with each other, in order to coordinate.
- Global coherence requires **global intimacy.**
- Global intimacy requires, like intimacy in any relationship, **a shared Story of Value.**

But in the two failed love stories of *Barbie* and Hamas, there is no shared Story of Value.

There is *a degraded, demonized value* of fundamentalism, and there is *a desiccated, disqualified value* of postmodernism.

Barbie and Hamas, both swelling movements in the world, postmodernity against fundamentalism, are both failed love stories. We don't have a shared Story of Value.

Only a shared Story of Value can respond to existential risk, which is the death of humanity or the death of *our* humanity.

A disqualified value produces the military-industrial complex, but it also produces TechnoFeudalism, a technocratic totalitarianism—a structure designed to undermine free will, and to undermine choice, and to appeal to the lowest common denominator of human beings.

And then you have the fundamentalist position with its demonization of desire, and all of its utter horror.

That's why failed love stories are so dangerous.

So what's the response? The response has to be a third way. And the third way, the third possibility, this new allurement, is the realization that—

- The Universe is a love story,
- Eros is the ground of Reality. Reality is Eros, and Eros is the value of Reality.
- Reality seeks value. Reality has an appetite for value.
- Reality is desire—Eros and intimacy seeking ever deeper uniqueness, ever deeper diversity, and then ever larger unions from that diversity, and ever deeper goodness, truth, and beauty.

How do we know that the Universe is a love story? Let's look at the Hebrew name of God, a four-letter name of God, from right to left it reads, *Yod Hei Vav Hei:*

יהוה

Hei Vav Hei Yod

Going from right to left (as we read in Hebrew):

- The *Yod* enters the *Hei*. *Yah*, as in Leonard Cohen, *Hallelu-yah*. The breath of Reality is the *Yod* entering the *Hei* in mad Eros.
- And then the *Vav* enters the *Hei*, the third letter enters the *Hei*, again in mad Eros.

The *Yod* entering the *Hei* is called **the *constant* Eros of Cosmos:** electromagnetism, gravitational allurement, the strong and weak nuclear forces, the structure of Reality.

And the *Vav* entering the *Hei* is called **the *aroused* Eros of Cosmos** in the *interior sciences*. The aroused Eros is the Eros generated by that same quality of allurement and desire, but now operating at the depths of human self-reflective consciousness.

In the interior sciences, meaning the deepest reading of all the traditional religions and all wisdom streams, Reality is the names of God, which is just another way of saying that:

- Reality is allurement.
- Reality is Eros.
- Reality is desire, and desire means: I am seeking value. I am desiring ever greater value.
- Reality has *an appetite*, wrote Whitehead, for value.

That's a love story.

The Universe is a love story.

The Universe is animated by desire—so I can trust my desire, and my desire tells me truth. I can trust my body. Do you feel that?

The book of Job, as it's read by the interior sciences, says, in Chapter 19: "Through my body, I vision God." Meaning, *I can trust my body.*

The stirrings of desire in my body—not in their pseudo-erotic form, not in their addictive form, not in their broken form, but my *clarifi*ed desire—**discloses value.**

- It is my desire for creativity.
- It is my desire for caring.
- It is my desire for nurturing.
- It is my desire for responsibility.
- It is my desire for aliveness.
- It is my desire for union.
- It is my desire for ever deeper intimacies, for ever deeper truth-telling, for ever deeper transformation, for ever deeper uniqueness.

These are the First Principles and First Values of Cosmos, which are the first *desires* of Cosmos. The first desires of Cosmos are its First Values, and the whole thing is a love story, which is why one text says:

Histakel b'oraita: she looked in the text, and the text is the names of God.

U'bara alma: the world is an expression of the names of God.

Meaning: Reality is desire. God is Eros, all the way up and all the way down. We are unique participatory expressions of the Field of Eros—Unique Selves, unique qualities, unique incarnations of intimacy and desire.

That's a love story—and ethos comes from that love story.

When there is no love story, when Eros is not a value, you have emptiness and you have pseudo-eros. Whether it's the postmodern version of pseudo-eros, or the fundamentalist version of pseudo-eros, they both produce destruction.

Our response has to be the overriding moral imperative of this time, like it was for da Vinci and Ficino, at the *Florentine Platonic Academy* in the *Renaissance,* which was also *a time between worlds and a time between stories.*

In this moment, in this breach, we have to—not just *tell,* not just *declare,* but *articulate, research, deepen, write, clarify*—the evolution of the human story, which is:

- Reality is a love story.
- No one is outside of the love story.

- Love is a value of Cosmos, and ErosValue a value of Cosmos.
- We all participate in that love story.
- We all have unique contributions to that love story.
- That love story is evolving, it is clarifying all the time.

That's The Universe: A Love Story.

That love story has to be so powerful, and so pulsing, and so throbbing—

- That it awakens Barbie and Ken;
- That actually, a Hamas apostate—the person who leaves Hamas— doesn't become a postmodernist, which is what's happening now.

Those who leave Hamas, go to Europe and become postmodern apostates, because the choice is either Hamas or postmodernism.

No, we have to *initiate* Reality, as da Vinci and Ficino did, into this new love story, grounded in the best of the interior and the exterior sciences.

That's where we're going. That's what we are here to do.

Is it *Barbie* or is it *Hamas?*

No, it is The Universe: A Love Story.

CHAPTER 14

THE STORY WE NEED
TO TELL

So now we know what we have to do, and we're going to close here. What a beautiful ride we did together. We're not just gaining information, but we are as revolutionaries, doing what they did in Florence, doing what they did in Mecca in the best of moments, doing what they've done in Jerusalem: we're telling this new story from around the world.

We've stayed in together. We've told this story. We've looked at this text of culture. We've unpacked this text of culture. We've looked at it carefully. We begin the telling of a new story. That's an incredibly beautiful thing to do. Because there's a gorgeous love story in the world.

Barbie and Ken need to come back together.

We need to re-embrace the Field of Desire as part of the Field of the Divine, as part of the field of *hieros gamos,* as part of the Field of God and Goddess.

Think back 20 years ago in your life, or 30 years ago in your life. It was a given in the world that:

- Great sexing should happen between beloveds.

- There's a right context for desire—whatever you think the right context is.
- The great and gorgeous expression of human desire in the Field of Eros is a self-evidently valid, gorgeous, wondrous expression of being alive.

This was a given. It's a great accomplishment to have wonderful and gorgeous and stunning Eros and to be in the living Field of Desire with whomever your beloved is. **It was a self-evident, self-validating truth of Cosmos.**

That is no longer the case.

Now, if there's no Field of Value, even sex is no longer a value. The essential notion that great sex, whatever that means, has value, doesn't exist anymore. Great sex used to mean something. It used to be part of this larger Field of Eros and desire. It's not. **Even the notion that people want to come together in sexing is rejected by the *Barbie* movie.** Barbie says, "We have no genitals."

But the point is that **the sexual is actually an intersubjective relationship between parts,** desperate to participate in each other, and to become part of a larger whole—**and that itself is the storyline of Cosmos.**

Even when I'm engaged in pleasuring by myself I'm accessing the larger Field of ErosPleasure and I'm pouring it back into the larger Field of ErosDesire. **When we dissociate from that field, we're left with nothing.** *Aphrodite dies.* That's unimaginable.

TO NOAH AND GRETA: LET'S MAKE MOVIES DRIPPING WITH EROS

I took this movie just as a random movie. I could have taken five others, just to point to this notion that:

- The love story has died.

- There's no notion of The Universe: A Love Story, it doesn't exist,
- We don't have a response to where or who or what *ought* be done.
- We are living in a world which is a desiccated world, which there's no ought, and which intentionally seeks to undermine the very notion that Reality is Eros is at the very center of culture.

Now it's not because there's bad people doing it, there's great people doing it. I want to be clear about that. I'm sure Noah and Greta (the writers of *Barbie*) are fantastic. But Noah and Greta could have done something else. And I hope they will in the future.

Noah and Greta could have done the rebellion against the old structures, against the old Barbie song. They could have taken on the best of the dogmatic positions of premodernity. **They could have taken on the best assumptions of modernity, and they could have participated in articulating a new story of desire.**

That's audacious movie-making. That's hot. That's something exciting. That's compelling. That has us awake and alive, tumescent and throbbing and yearning to actually speak and tell a new story.

What we need Noah and Greta to do is *participate*. First up, sweethearts, sit and study yourselves for a second. Get some depth yourselves, access sacred texts. Do study. Do practice. Get off the kind of win/lose metrics driving Hollywood: *Let's create another movie and succeed*. No, let's *study*, let's *go deep*, and then let's make movies.

Let's make movies that are dripping with Eros, but that are telling a new Story of Desire. Let's write a new *Song of Songs*.

Let's write a new love story. Let's write new Outrageous Erotic Love Letters.

- Let's recreate a world, which is the post-pornographic universe, which is tumescent and throbbing and alive and in which all of Reality is moving towards the most radically alive, ecstatic, pleasurable, complex, intimate communion, in all the ways of desire, in all the ways of sexing, and in which sexing is a value and desire is a value and all forms of desire are a value.

- Let's recreate a world in which each of us are unique configurations of desire, each of us are needed in a love story, and our love story is *chapter and verse* in the larger love story.

That's an exciting story.

Let's make a movie that actually blows Cosmos out of the water that you can watch in China, and you can watch in Africa, and **you can watch any place in the world and you say:**

"*Fuck*! That's what it means to be a human being."

The best of existentialism. The best of the great traditions. We weave it together. We tell a new story.

That's what we want to do.

YOUR NEED IS MY ALLUREMENT

I just touched the bare surface of this. We could go on for hours, without hyperbole, and take you through scene after scene after scene after scene.

I'll just give you the last image.

I'm just going to pick this one because it's so innocuous—so subtle, so easy to miss.

Remember that moment in the beginning of the movie, where there are flat feet, cellulite, death?

What Is Barbie's response? She's embarrassed.

What's the response of the other Barbies and Kens? They retch. They're disgusted.

Remember, what are we disgusted by?

Mortality.

But not only disgusted, we are *shamed* by our mortality. The reason sexuality, and sex, and death are so intimately related is because they both take us back to this animal dimension that, at least from the perspective of this world, dies. We are shamed by our mortality.

We are shamed by three things:

- We're shamed by **humiliation**, when we attempt to get our basic needs met.
- We're shamed by **death,** by our mortality.
- And we're shamed by our **powerlessness.**

But at its core, it's all about the shame of powerlessness. Barbie is embarrassed by death. She is ashamed.

This is this quality of shame that we're trying to avoid at all costs. But the only way to transpose shame is to realize that **in the depth of my being, my needs are filled with dignity.** My needs are not met with *shame* and *powerlessness.*

When we love each other madly, we look into each other's eyes, and we say, *Your need is my allurement.*

Isn't that beautiful?

Lovers look into each other's eyes, and they say, *Your need is my allurement.*

The act of sexing is when the lovers say to the beloved, *Your need is my allurement.*

It's why in sex we can heal the shame, which is the original shame of being humiliated in having my basic needs met.

But when I enter the world of sexing, and if I am madly on the inside with my beloved, I have this insatiable need that would cause me radical shame anyplace else in social discourse, and my lover looks at me, and she/he says, without words, *Your need is my allurement.*

Ken and Barbie, all the way up and all the way down the evolutionary chain.

Now imagine, my friends, if we said, *Your need is my allurement* not just to our one beloved?

- What if we moved beyond our one beloved, and we included the family, or the whole egocentric circle of intimacy, and said to our whole **egocentric circle of intimacy**, *Your need is my allurement?*
- What if we expanded that circle to ethnocentric intimacy, and we said to everybody in our *gang* and our nation—or whatever it is, whatever our larger gang is—*Your need is my allurement?*
- What if we went to worldcentric intimacy?
- And then to cosmocentric intimacy?

Do you see the line moving, and the circle expanding?

What if we said to every human being:

If you're hungry, I'm hungry.

If you're ripped apart, I'm ripped apart.

If you have no drinking water, I have no drinking water.

If your children are malnourished, I'm malnourished.

I was talking to my dear friend the other day. Someone close to him is dealing with a particular issue. He was talking to me about medical care. I said to my friend, how stunningly beautiful it is that they can go from this best doctor to that best doctor to get the best medical care.

Now, how much of the rest of the world has that available to them?

Your need is my allurement.

I can't sleep at night if people are hungry.

I can't sleep at night if 2 billion people in the world have no access to drinking water.

Your need is my allurement.

We are in the same circle of value.

OUTRAGEOUS ACTS OF LOVE

You might say, "Okay, that's too *fucking* big. What can I do with that?"

So here it is. We are going to close with this.

Why do we close our hearts?

If we are emerging as *Homo amor* we say:

- I am a love story,
- I'm CosmoErotic Universe in person,
- I realize Reality is a love story,
- *"Your need is my allurement"* extends to every human being on the planet.
- Maybe I even go to *cosmocentric intimacy* and feel every animal, and I actually feel the Cosmos itself, and I feel the past, the present, and the future, alive and awake in me.

If I feel the whole thing, then **what do I do with that?**

As my friend said to me yesterday, "How do I feel this much?"

When I feel too much I close down, because I can't hold it. It's not because I'm egocentric or narcissistic. It's because the gap between my ability to feel and my ability to heal is too great. In that gap, I close my heart.

So, how do I open my heart?

I can only open my heart if I close that gap. **Homo amor has to know how to close the gap.**

So here it is, and this is where we conclude.

Here's how we close the gap between our ability to feel and our ability to heal.

I say:

I am in relationship to the whole thing. I am willing to feel the whole thing—not every minute of every day, but I'm going to be in a relationship to the whole. The meta-crisis is a crisis of intimacy, and intimacy is our capacity to feel the whole.

Now, a thousand years ago, a very narrow band of enlightened people could feel the whole. But now, the notion of locality literally doesn't exist anymore. A virus infects the entire world. The notion of *only* local literally does not exist anymore.

It's not just one love; it is that one love is instantiated in a Reality that's completely interdependent.

So I have to be in a relationship to the whole. It's like when we see a picture of planet Earth, from Apollo, and realize, *Oh my god, that's us.* To be *Homo amor* is to be in a relationship to the whole. I experience the entire field.

Now, I cannot *heal* the whole.

So my next step is:

> I'm not just the True Self, I don't just feel the whole, I am Unique Self—and I don't need to heal everything. That is not my responsibility. I cannot do that. That's not mine to do.
>
> So what is mine to do?
>
> What's mine to do is answer the question *Who are you? Who am I?* (I apologize for using the word *you* but by *you*, I mean, *me* and *we*.)
>
> **Who are you?**
>
> You are an irreducibly unique expression of LoveIntelligence, and LoveBeauty, and LoveDesire of All-That-Is that lives in you, as you and through you that never was, is, or will be ever again, other than through you.

And as such, you, me, we, Unique Self Symphony, have the capacity to stand on the abyss of darkness and say, "Let there be light."

How?

Through living in my unique perspective and my unique quality of intimacy that come together to form my unique gifts that address a unique need in my unique circle of intimacy and influence.

That's what's mine to do.

To be a Unique Self means I have a unique set of allurements. It means I have a unique set of Outrageous Acts of Love that are mine to do and no one else's.

That's it.

I commit my Outrageous Acts of Love.

But I can't do it myself, so I look for others, because I am in a Unique Self Symphony.

I am going to find the others.

I am going to create the relationships that allow us to come together as Unique Self Symphonies, and commit Outrageous Acts of Love—not as a top-down organized surveillance structure, but as Unique Self Symphonies.

We begin to experience a Planetary Awakening in Evolutionary Love through Unique Self Symphonies—all the way up and all the way down.

Wow. That is a valid, compelling, and actually pragmatically available social vision.

We enact a world where I know who I am—and it's at the core structure and fabric of the education system itself.

Who am I? I am Unique Self.

I have a unique set of allurements.

I am a unique expression of the whole.

I have a unique gift to give to my unique circle of intimacy and influence.

Who are we? We are *Homo amor*.

Homo amor is the LoveIntelligence of Cosmos arising in me, as me, and through me—and then as we find each other in Unique Self Symphonies.

So what do I do? I do only what's mine to do.

But when I do what's mine to do, I love it open, I give it all.

It's mine and no one else is going to do this. I can't turn away. I step in.

To be a Unique Self is to be an Outrageous Lover. It's to feel Outrageous Love moving through me.

What does an Outrageous Lover do?

An Outrageous Lover keeps all the boundaries that should be kept and breaks all the boundaries that should be broken—and he/she commits Outrageous Acts of Love.

Then I realize, *Oh, that's why I'm here.* It's my greatest joy.

I commit Outrageous Acts of Love—for myself.

I love myself madly.

I love you madly because the whole thing is a love story.

The Universe is a love story.

Love is real.

Barbie and Ken are real.

It's real.

It's the most real thing that exists.

INDEX

www.ingramcontent.com/pod-product-compliance
Lightning Source LLC
LaVergne TN
LVHW011321080426
835513LV00006B/150